Beyond Capitalism?

The Future of Radical Politics

Beyond Capitalism?

The Future of Radical Politics

Luke Cooper & Simon Hardy

Winchester, UK
Washington, USA

First published by Zero Books, 2012
Zero Books is an imprint of John Hunt Publishing Ltd., Laurel House, Station Approach,
Alresford, Hants, SO24 9JH, UK
office1@jhpbooks.net
www.johnhuntpublishing.com
www.zero-books.net

For distributor details and how to order please visit the 'Ordering' section on our website.

A CIP catalogue record for this book is available from the British Library.

Design: Stuart Davies

Printed and bound by CPI Group (UK) Ltd, Croydon, CR0 4YY

We operate a distinctive and ethical publishing philosophy in all
areas of our business, from our global network of authors to
production and worldwide distribution.

CONTENTS

Thanks to friends and comrades for their inspiration
and help with this book

"Come, my friends,
'Tis not too late to seek a newer world."
Ulysses by Alfred Tennyson

Challenges for a new left

Has capitalism lost its capacity for internal renewal – to reform under the pressures of its own crises and antagonisms? Speaking back in 1996 on his book, *The Future of Capitalism,* Lester Thurow reflected on how social progress had been achieved in the 20th century. He anticipated that the decline of left wing politics would prove to be a problem for capitalism:

> What does a society do when problems start emerging, like falling wages in the United States, yet nobody has any idea about the alternative [to the status quo]? Suppose you didn't believe in capitalism, well what do you believe in? The answer is you wouldn't have anything to believe in anymore. And that means the dominant system, capitalism, loses the ability to reform itself. [Because]... if you look at the reforms made to capitalism over the last hundred and forty years, things like pensions, healthcare, unemployment insurance, they were all done under the pressure of socialists who said 'if you don't do this we're going to take over', whereas there is no one about to take over anymore.[1]

If we look at the reactions of global elites to the financial crisis since the collapse of Lehman Brothers, we can see visibly how Thurow's prophecy has been realised. Today, capitalism lacks an "other" in the sense of an opposition that it could define itself in relation to and which could, in turn, by appearing to threaten the system's existence, compel ruling elites to reform and attempt to overcome the internal contradictions of the system. Thurow's argument remains powerful because it begs the question: what will capitalism look like as a system when it is 'left to its own devices', when it assumes such a degree of political authority that the cultural condition of humanity becomes ever more capitalistic? At times over the last decades capitalist ideology had *its own utopia* – i.e. an idealised vision of the market-driven and technologically-refined society that globalisation was pushing us towards – but since the financial crisis it has lacked this certainty about the future it is creating.

At the same time, a credible left wing politics has also not emerged that might compel ruling elites to reform, in the manner that Thurow described occurring in the 20th century. This seemingly post-utopian conjuncture poses challenges to those who still argue for going "beyond capitalism". For radical leftists that believe there *is indeed an alternative*, the challenge is how do we make this idea credible again? And even if it does become credible once more, how can we stop capitalism from incorporating aspects of our project into its own reproduction as a profit-driven system? The capitalist crisis poses profound questions about the future of left wing politics because of its sheer depth and severity. When leading establishment think tanks anticipate *decades* of austerity will be the norm in a number of western countries,[2] then it brings to light the epochal nature of the current crisis – of how the changes which are forged out of this cauldron of discontent will determine the future for a much longer period ahead. While the longevity of the crisis underlines the scope for preparation and the gradual marshalling of support amongst wider layers of working class people, the crisis nonetheless still poses sharply the 'if not now – then when?' question for anticapitalist and socialist activists. After all, in these conditions radical political ideas should be striking a chord amongst millions of workers and, if they are not, then we have to look hard at ourselves. We have written this book as activists in the movement who want to reappraise some of the historical problems of the left in light of the transformations the world has undergone over the last three decades. Two themes occupy our attention in what follows. Firstly, we discuss the evolution of political life since the 1970s and the fate of the radical left after the neoliberal revolution. In most countries in the world not only is acceptance of capitalism fundamental to the assumptions of the major political parties, but a specific variant of neoliberal ideology has come to be seen as the exclusive road down which politics must travel. Of course there are variations and differences - we do not want at all to deny the fact that world capitalism remains a mosaic of enormous variety. Indeed, we admit that much of the narrative we tell might be based on a specific set of experiences in Anglo-American politics. But we do nonetheless believe there are general problems for the left in the post-1989 world, which we have to grapple with and understand if we are to find a way forward.

The second theme of our book might appear more distant and more abstract, yet it cuts to the core of how political struggle and resistance is formed today. How do we move beyond capitalism? Or, even, whether it is *possible* to move beyond capitalism? How we choose to answer these questions has strategic consequences. Historically, most discussion on the radical left deals with this second question and explores a spectrum of possibilities. If we consider the programmes that emerged in the post-war period until the 1980s, then there were several specific strategies which were each in their own way considered by large numbers of people to be a viable means through which capitalism could ultimately be transcended: parliamentary reformism, peasant insurrection, Autonomism and urban guerrilla-ism, and a party-led working class insurrection *à la* the October Revolution.

While these movements were diverse – and each ideology gained a foothold amongst sections of society at different points in space and time – they each contributed to the general conception of the 20th century as a great tussle between capitalism and its left-modernist challengers. The post-1989 world is strikingly different in this regard, and so, to speak of radical change at all, almost recalls a bygone age. An 'elephant in

3

the room' problem – so often occluded or just downplayed in left wing discussion – that imposes itself on activists, is that to arrive at a conjuncture where anticapitalist strategies can be implemented will require an extraordinary transformation in the consciousness of millions.

The gap between *where we are* and *where we want to be* is the basic problematic of left politics today. Once you get passed the optimistic rhetoric of the left, the fear that lingers behind the scenes is whether we can overcome the radical disjuncture between our political aspirations and the degree of support in the working class that genuine revolutionary change requires. This problem is not entirely novel, because of the first of our questions – how we analyse society – has always informed perspectives on how to change it. Many radicals in the 1960s responded to an apparent decline in left wing radicalism by searching out 'new revolutionary subjects' beyond the working class as it was traditionally understood. Bold and imaginative as these endeavours often were, they failed to build movements that had the social power to realise the anti-systemic goals they held to. In their impatience they tended to isolate the most radical from orgainsed labour and so allowed its reformist ethos to go relatively unchallenged. But they nonetheless emerged out of a real problem: bureaucratisation had rendered the labour movement passive and conservative.

Today, we are still in a period marked by the long-term decline of organised forms of radical left wing politics. The problem is all the worse if we consider how proletarian revolutionaries, with no support amongst the proletariat, can often be a staple of establishment humour. Comrade Wolfie, an urban guerrilla in Tooting, from the 1970s TV show *Citizen Smith* famously encapsulated this. The joke (all too familiar, unfortunately) was that he spoke a language and led a lifestyle that workers could not understand, let alone relate to. So his claim to 'leadership' was literally farcical. Reversing the trend to isolation, still to this day expressed in the cultural idiosyncrasies of the left, is perhaps the central question facing activists in the 21st century. Answering it will arguably require a critical appraisal of our existing understanding of how to make the bridge 'to the masses'.

The experience of isolation from the working class is however complex. It is not simply through denial that the revolutionary left 'carry on regardless' – emphasising the positive and building trade union and social struggles – but there is in fact a real disjuncture between their daily political practice and wider ideology. Socialists can often find themselves at the centre of social movements. We saw this during the student revolt and in the role the organised left played in building demonstrations and strikes in Britain across 2011 activists. The contradiction lies in how Trotskyist or Leninist tradition will be respected for their activism *despite* their wider ideology and this can breed complacency and routinism on the left, because all things being equal it should be facing up to a crisis that goes to the heart of its very existence as a left. But the sense of exhilaration that comes with movement-building puts the left on life support. We are happy to build the next demonstration without having to wrestle with the knottier issue of how to render the anticapitalist and revolutionary politics properly "organic" to these social movement mobilisations.

While the revolutionary socialist left tends to look to the Bolshevik model of party organisation as their template, their understanding of what it means in practice – the formation of small disciplined cadre organisations fighting for a narrowly defined strategy in the movement – does not properly accord with the totality of the Russian experience. It overlooks how the Bolsheviks *emerged out of* an attempt to construct a party, defined politically in broadly Marxist terms, which could achieve socialist hegemony over the working class. The Bolshevik tradition tends to be read as a history of splits 'from above' – i.e. as arguments amongst the leading Russian Marxists – rather than 'from below' in the forms of political organisation that were established within the Russian working class. Achieving a greater degree of unity is arguably one of the pressing questions facing the radical left today because, compared to the Russian Social Democratic Labour Party, its organisational divisions, at least in most countries of the world, are numerous and badly undermine its ability to instil an anticapitalist consciousness in wider society.

A sombre comparison between the dramatic growth of the radical left after 1968 and the much more modest gains made after the mass movements of 2011 underline the fact that Marxism has lost its position as the natural 'go-to politics' for radicals in struggle today. Quite simply people are not joining the organised left in the way that they used to and we need to start appraising why this is in more practical terms. A start would be to ask people who participated in these movements why they were not joining the Marxist left, and then to think about whether these were real principled differences or whether they just had concerns about secondary questions. If it turns out to be the latter, then the radical left has a duty to reflect on these criticisms and think about how it can become more attractive.

Indeed, one problem with the theoretical output of the organised revolutionary left is its propensity to find excuses for its marginalisation from wider society and, in the process, try and justify practices that "common sense" typically questions. Each socialist group will tend to explain the disunity of the left as justified on the basis of the differences which exist amongst its various constituent parts instead of asking if, at least some of, these differences could co-exist within a common organisation. Low levels of radicalisation are explained by the use of universal generalisations about "leadership" or "confidence", without appraising the more specific and concrete challenges and *our own* failures as a left to develop a socialist politics that really resonates. Marginalisation can breed a *de facto* reliance on official leaders of the unions, justify opportunism towards them on the grounds of realism (that in effect accept as 'realistic' what they say), and focus energy away from the longer-term need for independent, grassroots organisation of trade union members. And the list could go on. All of these positions each contain elements of truth – for instance, it would be wrong to never work with a union official or make unrealistic demands on union members – but their overall logic is to justify conservatism and sectarianism, and their purpose is to explain away the failure to connect socialist ideas to real people. If, in contrast, we accept that the gap between our intentions and the reality of our circumstances has become unbearable, then it can open up avenues for fresh thinking about how to bridge this gap between aspiration and reality. In short, recognising the problem might be a condition for going forward. It is our contention, put across in the closing chapters, that a bit more 'common sense' – in the sense of *practice-informed strategic politics* – could go a long way to improving the radical left.

This might sound pessimistic; perhaps even the normal impatience and frustrations of the intelligentsia. However, we explore these points across the following chapters not from the standpoint of critical observers, but as activists on the radical left. We first came into the movement during the 'summit sieges' that took off with the Seattle protests in 1999 and have drawn these conclusions from our experience in left wing politics since. This was far from entirely negative, but we do believe there are fundamental problems that require re-evaluation on the part of all activists. The opportunities we have in front of us make reappraising the received wisdoms of a marginalised left all the more pressing.

Perhaps we should see the resistance of 2011 as having opened up two roads for the left. In one direction there lies further isolation and with it the assertion, ever-more categorically and trenchantly, of the theoretical justifications for our position. But down the other road, should we choose by our own free volition to take it, lies the possibility of renewal and progress, if, that is, we grasp the opportunity that the economic crisis presents to actually destabilise and reshape Marxism into a meaningful and resolutely *practical* politics.

We could do much worse than learning from how neoliberalism was able to achieve its ideological hegemony over the last decades. It managed to sustain the idea that marketisation was synonymous with progressive ideals: the expansion of democracy and human freedom and modernity as a vision of ascending technological and social progress. The current economic crisis has, in part at least but not entirely, broken these planks of neoliberal ideology. The prospect of decades of austerity leaves its claim to represent social progress badly undermined. Growing public awareness of the myriad of corrupt ties between each of the central pillars of capitalist hegemony – the rich, media, police, and politicians – has also dented its democratic credibility. But if there is an opportunity to be seized with this decline, the lesson of its original genesis continues to hold true: the left must make the ideals of progress and modernity, and democracy and freedom, its own. Indeed, they must become an organic part of the renewal of a practical Marxist politics.

1989 and 2011: the new global revolutions or 'we are all liberals now'?

Reflections on 2011 share a common conviction that it was one of those 'mad years' – when a series of uprisings and revolutions that were dispersed across the globe with apparently distinct causes intersected with one another and fed into a general sense of social upheaval in world politics. 1848, 1917, 1968, 1989 are all identified as conjunctures of a similar magnitude; when changes that once appeared impossible suddenly seem inevitable.

Time will tell whether 2011 does go down in history as such a decisive conjuncture that foreshadowed decades of social change.

But the movements of 2010 – 2011 have certainly shifted the terrain of possibilities for the radical left. Revolutions against despots in the Middle East and North Africa and the rise of large-scale anti-austerity movements in Western Europe intersected with the structural crisis and instability in the global economy. These have not only seen traditional labour movement protests, but also the more overtly political call of #Occupy for a new kind of politics based on the 99%; a movement that represented a powerful ideological challenge to thirty years of economic policy in the West.

Recent developments have also produced a shift in the psychology of ruling elites. As Paul Mason has argued, the post-2008 recession has brought to earth with a bump the neo-conservative outlook on social change that was once perfectly summarised by Karl Rove's riposte to the academic world as the 'reality-based community':

That's not the way the world works anymore. We're an empire now, and when we act, we create our own reality. And while you're studying that reality – judiciously as you will – we'll act again creating other new realities, which you can study too, and that's how things will sort out. We're history actors... and you, all of you, will be left to just study what we do.[3]

This idea of neoliberal governments in the West as seemingly all-powerful 'change makers' has, since the crisis broke in 2008, been displaced by a new collective psychology which sees the same economic agenda pursued through a series of political *reactions* to the unfolding crisis. The change in outlook is typified by the Eurozone crisis. At its foundation no constitutional mechanism was established that would allow states to leave the Euro but remain in the European Union, because the failure of the project was simply not considered possible. Now, however, the prospect of states leaving the Eurozone – and all the emergency constitutional measures that would require – is a really quite tangible possibility. Should it happen it is unlikely to involve careful planning by elites, but will be a consequence of an economic breakdown in one or other of the most-indebted states. In any case, this underlines the reactive and uncertain nature of today's neoliberal policy making.

The new revolutions of 2011 may appear to have come seemingly out of nowhere, but these kinds of turning points in history will always bring to the surface of events long-maturing contradictions and processes. To understand them we need to keep in mind what the sociologist Fernand Braudel called "the dialectic of duration", "the living and continuous tension between the moment and the span of time".[4] Braudel meant that in a single moment of time a vast array of historical experiences become concentrated. Such "multiple and contradictory timespans of the lives of men" are "not only the substance of the past but also the stuff of present social life."[5] Any single conjuncture "builds upon" the accumulated experiences of the past and these historical episodes continue to resonate into the present.

If we consider the great turning points in history (1848, 1917, 1968, etc.) in such terms, then each one can be seen as adding new experiences and realities to the modern world. Each of these years are identified with revolutionary movements that appeared at one time to threaten capitalism but then had their utopia 'otherised' and the immediate programmes co-opted into the lifecycle of the system. In 1848 it was revolutionary democracy, as mass urban-based movements demanded that power pass from the old elites to the people. In 1917 the overthrow of Tsarism unleashed communism onto the world stage, compelling reforms from ruling elites who suddenly felt their social power threatened, as well as stimulating the rise of openly totalitarian anti-Bolshevik movements on the political right. And in 1968, a diverse series of elements – from anti-Stalinist Marxism, to feminism, black liberation and revivified labour struggles – demanded the social freedoms of the oppressed and an egalitarian redistribution of the fruits of post-war industrialisation in East and West. Seen in these terms, 1989 is novel because it was a crisis that exclusively took place 'within anti-capitalism' rather than its antagonists. Or, at least, it came to be seen as such, and thus laid the basis for an unprecedented expansion in the hegemony of liberalism.

We cannot understand the meaning, let alone the potential, of 2011 without recognising the challenge it represents to the fabric of the 'post-Berlin Wall world'. The years from the collapse of Lehman Brothers in 2008 through to the Arab Spring of 2011 saw the rupturing of the key ideological and economic assumptions of the international order; that globalisation and technological transformation would bring prosperity and development to every corner of the globe. By undermining the idealistic claims of neo-conservatism and its proponents' feeling of omnipotence, a space has opened up in mass society to contest this way of organising political and economic life. But it is only a partial rupture - a destabilisation of the old ways – because the continuity also remains striking. The fiscal measures of western states are designed precisely to sustain systems of neoliberal accumulation to which ruling elites are still committed. Resistance movements that contest this still remain largely within the assumptions of liberal democratic ideology. This is the key challenge that confronts any attempt to develop a more generalised anticapitalist response to the current social crisis. It can be summed up with the question: 'are we all liberals now?'

The economic crisis has had an over-determining impact on global politics in the sense that its effects are felt in every aspect of our culture, but its contradictions can arguably only find their resolution at the level of politics. Leon Trotsky's observation, following the economic downturn interlaced with political and social upheavals after the First World War, that the tasks of the economic base are "submitted for solution in the sphere of the superstructure"[6] powerfully resonates with today's conjuncture. For the central antagonism that cuts through society is that between governments (i.e. the "political superstructure") trying to sustain the neoliberal accumulation model at "the base", and the contestation of this programme by political and social movements "from below". The slowly emerging and tentative rival of anticapitalist consciousness amongst layers of society that go far beyond the left – expressed in everyday reactions to corruption scandals, tax cuts for the rich and the use of the unemployed as free labour in social security schemes – indicates the possibilities for a more far reaching renewal of radical politics. But there remains a disjuncture between this consciousness and attempts to give it an active, political expression. The "old hierarchies", be it the European social democracy or conservative organisations like the Muslim Brotherhood in the Arab Spring, still have a reach and depth of social support that is far beyond anything the political left can muster.

The perspective of a prolonged phase of economic crisis and social convulsion is commonly shared on the left and not without justification. For all the uncertainty of the current moment, a long-period of sluggish growth and crises can be anticipated for the simple reason that the western economies remain shackled by debt and its governments are almost universally committed to propping up the financial interests that own these credit assets. Although the costs of this will be distributed unevenly across Europe, the working classes generally face a deepening of austerity. The effect of which can be summed up as an attack on what the European left call "the social wage". That is, a forcing downwards not only of wages, but also of the proportion of wealth generated in society which is used to fund the social security, health, education and welfare benefits of the labouring masses. In some countries, particularly Britain, the heartland of neoliberalism, this goes alongside a dramatic programme of *de facto* privatisation, which opens up core welfare services to private sector tendering, and so creates, through bureaucratic means, unprecedented avenues for tax payers' money to find its way into the pockets of profit-making companies. While this is a continuation of neoliberal dogma (markets are good, state monopolies are bad), it is hardly a picture of the nimbler and dynamic market against the slothful state. Highly complex bureaucratic systems – such as the British governments' new structure for the National Health Service – are actually created to manage this transfer of funds to private hands. Added to this is the depression-like economic context for these measures that has seen a return of structurally high unemployment with its disciplining logic on the employed: "Don't like it? Well, there are ten other people on the dole who would happily do your job".

Indeed, the optimistic hubris that surrounded the march of globalisation has given way to a new climate of immense pessimism and a crisis of intellectual answers in the sphere of mainstream public policy. But government policy remains largely consistent with the previous three decades. A key feature of neoliberalism was always to favour the biggest sections of finance capital with banks in particular a highly privileged interest group. A key point of continuity between the pre and post 2008 world is to socialise the losses of the banks and defend the financialized wealth of the biggest blocs of international capital.

As David Harvey has argued, since the regulatory changes of the 1970s increased the danger of systemic-risk in the marketplace the state has been mobilised systematically – despite the liberal economic doctrine of non-interference in the markets – to defend financial interests:

One of the basic pragmatic principles that emerged in the 1980s, for example, was that state power should protect financial institutions at all costs. This principle, which flew in the face of the non-interventionism that neoliberal theory prescribed, emerged from the New York City fiscal crisis of the mid-1970s. It was then extended internationally to Mexico in the debt crisis that shook that country to the core in 1982. Put crudely, the policy was: privatise profits and socialise risks; save the banks and put the screws on the people (in Mexico, for example, the standard of living of the population dropped by about a quarter in four years after the financial bail-out of 1982). The result was what was known as 'systemic moral hazard'. Banks behave badly because they do not have to be responsible for the negative consequences of high-risk behaviour. The current bank bail-out is this same old story, only bigger and this time centred in the United States.[7]

Class interests have always stood behind the neoliberal restructuring of modern capitalism. It was never therefore simply a body of rational thought that rose on the basis of truth and evidence, and could fall just as easily once that evidence proved suspect, but it was, or rather it is, as Harvey has put it, a "project of ruling class power". Elsewhere, Harvey has described these interests groups as the "Party of Wall Street"[8] that successfully colonised Anglo-American political institutions regardless of election results.

If the capitalist politicians of our age were honest – quite an *if!* - and actually produced a "manifesto" of genuine intent, then what would it have in it? There are several key policies that are currently shared by the political elites across Europe and the United States.

1. Save the banking sector;
2. Open new markets to realise profits (privatisation, moderate or informal mercantalism);
3. Carry on the massive transfer of wealth from poor to rich,

ensuring sufficient capital for future investment when the economy picks up again;

4. Dismantle the welfare state/public sector in education, social provision and healthcare;

5. Discipline the workforce, end welfare and smash workers' rights;

6. As a by-product of these policies, creating mass unemployment that will help to further depress wages and discourage working class resistance.

One of the most important features of the economic tendencies established since the 1970s - the transfer of wealth from the poor to the rich – is a central feature of policy making and the economic motors of the global financial crisis. The accumulation of massive wealth in the hands of the 1% is a long-term feature of US policy-making. As Michael Moore has pointed out in his film *Capitalism: A Love Story*, the top rate of income tax was slashed by over 50 per cent – from 70 per cent in 1980 to 28 per cent in 1989 and, during the same decade government policies aggressively sought to raise by productivity through pushing down labour costs, resulting in stagnating incomes for American workers.[9] This same aggressively anti-labour policy has persisted throughout the last decade under both the Bush and Obama administration and even given an added intensity after the financial crisis of 2008. Between 2010 and 2012 the average pay of US CEOs increased by 14 per cent to some $12.9 million, an astonishing 380 times the average wage of US workers.[10]

After the banking crisis has been resolved and the austerity measures have reduced the social wage to manageable levels, the handful of people who financially benefited from the crisis will be in prime position to make a "killing" in new rounds of investment, capital restructuring, mergers and acquisitions, and privatisation. The wildfire now is to clear the forest for a future round of growth, one that will occur on the broken backs of the poor. This is how capitalism will survive, if everything goes "according to plan".

The current phase of capitalist development involves both an economic crisis and an ideological crisis, which goes to the central cultural assumptions of globalisation and neoliberalism. It can, thus, be described in the words of Gramsci as an "organic crisis":

> In every country the process is different, although the content is the same. And the content is the crisis of the ruling class's hegemony, which occurs either because the ruling class has failed in some major political undertaking for which it has requested, or forcibly extracted, the consent of the broad masses (war, for example), or because huge masses . . . have passed suddenly from a state of political passivity to a certain activity, and put forward demands which taken together, albeit not organically/formulated, add up to a revolution. A 'crisis of authority' is spoken of: this is precisely the crisis of hegemony, or 'general crisis of the state'. It consists precisely in the fact that the old is dying and the new cannot be born; in this interregnum a great variety of morbid symptoms appear.[11]

Organic crisis reverberate through society, exacerbating the social tensions, for injustices that were once considered "normal" and thus "containable" suddenly have an explosive quality. In August 2011, riots ripped through inner city Britain. Mostly young people, fed up with poverty and police harassment took their anger out on the shopping centres and on the police. Owen Hatherley summed up how this reflected a pent of rage against *a lack of resistance* to a crisis-ridden neoliberal capitalism that was "trying to commit suicide":

> Over the last few years, the ruling class has kept trying to

commit suicide—financial crisis, expenses scandal, News International, the Met, financial crisis mark two—and most of us won't let them. We'd rather Keep Calm and Carry On. These kids, venal and stupid as some of their actions obviously are, don't want to carry on. They want to see the whole bloody thing burn.[12]

The riots saw visceral violence, looting (the desire to expropriate the trainers and plasma TVs of consumerist Britain), and expressed the utter alienation of a whole generation. Many of whom had, no doubt, participated in the student protests of winter 2010, as thousands of working class college students fought to keep their EMA and not be priced out of university.

Discipline and punishment, thus, have not simply arisen out of the logic of neoliberal labour-capital relations in the workplace, but also extended into the political sphere. Pressure for a sharpening of immigration controls, a rise of racist sentiment, and an increase in intrusive and intimidating police tactics, are all part of a picture of social unrest in Europe. In Britain, police have adopted forms of semi-paramilitary public order tactics that have long been the norm in Europe. Water-cannons and plastic bullets have been legalised and pre-emptive arrests have been carried out prior to protests "to prevent a breach of the peace".

These are all grim reminders of the failure of liberalism to deliver a utopian vision. As George Orwell once wrote, "if you want a picture of the future, imagine a boot stamping on a human face forever."[13] It is too easy to respond, "the boot has started stamping", but it certainly poses questions about whether the liberal centre can hold – especially in the European states that are the greatest victims of austerity economics. If civil-isation on this model requires a system of control and direction to protect civilisation from itself, then an issue of durability arises ineluctably. In many European states, it is the xenophobic far right and not the left that looks set to benefit from the real perception that the unaccountable and bureaucratic structures of liberal globalisation have failed 'the common man'. While this all might appear to be favourable to the renewal of organised anticapitalist politics on a wider basis amid this social instability and crises, plainly there are reactionary dangers here too and their spectre castes a long shadow over contemporary Europe. The possibility of another avenue – of an enduring but depoliticised neoliberal centre moving from crisis to crisis – was seen in the Murdoch affair of 2011-2012. On this path, the establishment becomes a regime of permanent crisis, but it lacks any kind of ideological challenge, so its crises become less and less political, more and more managerial, and so breeds apathy and cynicism at the base.

The existence of this enormous variety in possible outcomes – with all the contingencies involved in what path is eventually taken – underlines how there is no axiomatic relationship between economic instability and political consciousness. Its mediation through a variety of cultural conditions adds to the complexity of the current moment. While this is widely recognised by radicals, the logical consequence of it – that we need to think hard about how we get our "own house in order" on the left – is less acknowledged, let alone discussed.

While liberal capitalist society gropes towards a reorganisation that, it is hoped, will solve the structural problems that appear to be endemic to the system, the left needs to forge a new project. A project which can shift the balance of power towards an anticapitalist perspective, breaking the vicious circles we have fallen into and replacing them with new, dynamic and virtuous circles. Whether we win or lose the coming battles, the labour movement is in a process of change, of simultaneous decomposition and re-composition, and we have to find the mechanisms to help new layers of activists emerging through this process come into radical politics. For the left it is no problem to re-imagine, to re-conceive, the economic crisis as an opportunity for radical politics. While this might generate self-assurance and confidence, it is quite another thing to convince wider sections of the labour movement and young people that radical political change is becoming credible once again. To do this we will surely need to draw them into the process of actively developing a new and modern radical politics. A reflective and critical evaluation of long held orthodoxies and traditions is needed which can help foster new avenues for unity. A resolute focus on the conjuncture and its practical demands, a willingness to fraternally discuss 'old disagreements' in the context of on-going collaboration, must become the norm and not the exception. Our goal in writing *Beyond Capitalism? The Future of Radical Politics* is to begin an analytically-informed but thoroughly political debate on the left about how to move forward. We are sure that we do not have all the answers, but we believe that we have enough observations to begin a process of intellectual exchange and collaboration that can help us rise to the challenges of today.

Capitalist realism

The economic crisis that erupted in 2008 and the upsurge of global resistance to austerity have brought back into focus the simple fact we live in a system of capitalist production. But this in itself raises an even more pressing question: what alternative is there to capitalism? It is hard for us to even imagine what could possibly come after the present system.

One of the reasons the left has struggled to make inroads is that, while there is a new discussion opening amongst the political elite on the type of capitalism they want, the ruling class is still able to perpetuate the impression capitalism is "the only game in town".

This is what the cultural critic Mark Fisher describes as the problem of capitalist realism, which "refers to the widespread belief that there is no alternative to capitalism - though `belief' is perhaps a misleading term, given that its logic is externalised in the institutional practices of workplaces and the media as well as residing in the heads of individuals... This means that, however much individuals or groups may have disdained or ironised the language of competition, entrepreneurialism and consumerism that has been installed in UK institutions since the 1980s, our widespread ritualistic compliance with this terminology has served to naturalise the dominance of capital and help to neutralise any opposition to it."[14]

Perry Anderson, the editor of *New Left Review*, made a similar point in an editorial in 2000:

Ideologically, the novelty of the present situation stands out in historical view. It can be put like this. For the first time since the Reformation, there are no longer any significant opposi-tions — that is, systematic rival outlooks — within the thought-

world of the West; and scarcely any on a world scale either...
Whatever limitations persist to its practice, neo-liberalism as
a set of principles rules undivided across the globe: the most
successful ideology in world history.[15]

Alain Badiou the Marxist philosopher similarly conceded that,
"Today we see liberal capitalism and its political system, parlia-
mentarianism, as the only natural and acceptable solutions".[16]
The result is a continual lowering of our political horizons. For
the idea that society is moving forward, refining and improving
the human condition in that now much maligned classical sense
of "progress", is increasingly lost. These cultural tendencies are
particularly felt in the West, but the hold of capitalist liberalism
on social consciousness is arguably a global phenomenon. Even
in states such as China, whose political system is an enduring
relic of its Stalinist past, the direction of development is towards
greater liberalisation on free market lines – and the role of
capitalism as the modernising agent in society frames all its
political discourse. Here, given the dramatic industrial transformation China has achieved, the idea of progress and modernisation certainly persists, but it is understood in entirely capitalist
lines. Changes over the last two decades in China have been part
of a process of expanding capitalist globalisation, whose origins
lay twofold in the neoliberal revolution in the West and the
collapse of the USSR, allowing an unprecedented expansion in
the reach and power of market exigencies over the world.

Since Marx, radicals on the left have often been derided for
seeing economic crisis and social unrest as an opportunity for
sweeping political transformation. But the idea of a crisis "as an
opportunity riding a dangerous wind", as the famous Chinese
proverb put it, has long been recognised by ruling elites and
their ideologues in the West. Milton Friedman, a right wing
economist who spent his life fighting to dismantle the welfare
state, said of his own project that it would only come to fruition

in a time of great upheaval. "Only a crisis—actual or perceived — produces real change", he wrote, "When that crisis occurs, the actions that are taken depend on the ideas that are lying around. That, I believe, is our basic function: to develop alternatives to existing policies, to keep them alive and available until the politically impossible becomes politically inevitable."[17]

Friedman realised his project in his lifetime. Indeed, no account of the political and social transformations Margaret Thatcher achieved in Britain and Ronald Reagan similarly engineered in the United States can be complete without recognising the role played by thinkers like Friedman during the economic crisis of the 1970s. With the end of the post-war boom the economies of the West were wracked by high inflation and stagnant output. The squeeze on profits undermined the old politics of social compromise between capital and labour and saw rising industrial strife. It was during this time, that economists influenced classical liberal economic principles of *laissez faire* (the "market good, state bad" logic of neoliberalism), succeeded in winning a significant degree of political support amongst the ruling political elites, as their programme suddenly appeared to offer a credible alternative to the post-war economic paradigm.

The paradox of globalisation was the coexistence of social progress alongside growing social inequalities. Individuals did achieve greater freedoms and democratic rights in most states of the world as the Soviet Union fell and liberal democracy globalised. But only at the expense of allowing capital and finance an extraordinary mobility to seek out cheap labour markets, penetrate public services and create a growing race to the bottom. The East Asian sweatshop turning out Nike trainers became symbol of these transformations in the 1990s.

As Daniel Bensaid put it, the peculiarity of globalisation is that the internationalisation it achieved brought into question key foundational pillars of global capitalism:

The long epoch of political modernity that began with the English revolution of the seventeenth century. Under the impact of globalization, the classic categories of nation, people, sovereignty, citizenship, and international law have been called into question, without being replaced.[18]

The secret of how these changes became hegemonic globally lies in capitalist realism. The perception that "socialism had been defeated" intensified the tendency of capitalism to make markets appear natural, ever-present and not historically transient. By extending the naturalising tendencies of the market apparently anachronistic elements of society – such as nations, sovereignty, even citizenship – suddenly appeared to be fading away, but, so too did modernistic challengers to capitalism, such as the goal of socialist transformation.

Generally speaking, our sense of what is possible is powerfully conditioned by what already exists. Capitalism in particular is able to manipulate our *sense of time* in subtle but powerful ways. This might sound far-fetched, even the stuff of conspiracy, but, in fact, all dominant class structures in history have fostered the idea of being timeless and unchangeable. They are able to do this because of the contradictory way that we experience the passing of time. The past, present and future are familiar categories to us – but how we draw them together can be unstable and subject to many different influences. As social individuals our impressions of the past are formed through our collective activity with others. And our practical activity in the here and now looks towards a future that is necessarily uncertain to us, but also the subject of our aspirations. Our uncertain sense of time, about the past and the future, means that society continually shapes our ideas.

Marx observed that humanity makes history, "but they do not make it as they please; they do not make it under self-selected circumstances, but under... [those] already given and transmitted from the past". [19] It is these "transmitted conditions" that shape our existence and our sense of time. Class analysis in Marxism is well known, but it wasn't just class relations that Marx thought we inherited. He also saw our ideas and consciousness as a key part of our material existence too. The way we make sense of the world and one another, how we think about it, and how we describe it, has a direct impact on *what we do* to "make history". Consider, for instance, how important nationalism, let alone national identity, has been to shaping the modern world and how we think about our communities. Recognition of the influence of these socially constructed forms of consciousness had on our practice, led Marx to add that "the tradition of all dead generations weighs like a nightmare on the brains of the living".[20] His point was not simply that political practices of years gone past will affect how we resist today, but that it is difficult for us to even think in political terms outside of the inherited assumptions and traditions of our communities, as we nearly always define our politics in relation to our past experiences. This is a particular problem for progressive, i.e. forward looking, notions of political progress and human emancipation, because we are advocating a step into the unknown which exists in a certain tension to the 'normal' conception of politics as a series of traditions emerging out of past, lived experiences. Talk to activists on the very small and marginalised left wing of the Labour Party and you will see that this testifies to the enduring importance of Marx's point. They will tend to argue against an alternative to the Labour Party exclusively with reference to 'negative' past experiences of building alternatives; "it hasn't happened before, so it can't happen", so, in other words, the "traditions [and failures] of all dead generations [continue] to weigh live a nightmare on the brains of the living".

How the past "weighs like a nightmare on us" is also key to understanding how class systems are able to take advantage of our imperfect sense of time. Because we live *in the moment* our sense of the past, our "access to it" is formed out of collective memories. So, if a system can create the impression it is timeless, if it can appear as natural, then it can also appear to be indestructible. It can reinforce a sense that it is pervasive not only across space, but also across time. This sensibility alone, this collective feeling, can powerfully influence the way we act – even at moments of social breakdown and revolutionary crisis.

The results are not always negative. Consider how perceptions of the miners' strike that took place in Britain during 1984 and 1985 still have a grip on consciousness to this day, particularly in the north of England. When a group of ex-miners' wives organised a mock 'picket' of the *Iron Lady* film in Chesterfield, they weren't just driven by a memory, but by a shared sense of the legacy left behind by Thatcher's assault on working people. They were joined by younger people who could not have remembered the strike, but with government cuts hitting workers again today it is little wonder they targeted British Deputy Prime Minister Nick Clegg ("Clegg-y, Clegg-y, Clegg-y – out, out, out") as well as Thatcher.[21] When an alternative history is kept alive like this, it challenges the monopoly on history that ruling elites claim for themselves.

The power of capitalism lies in its ability to encourage forms of behaviour that sustain itself – even when its irrationality and injustice stands particularly exposed. Its secret lies in the way it combines a sense of our *personal independence* – a sense that we are free to do what we want with our lives – with a parallel *dependence* on the market to realise our "freedom".[22] We are so used to a system where we sell our labour for wages, where capitalists profit out of this work, and where we are dependent on the market to buy goods, that it is difficult for us to even imagine an alternative system. When the miners' wives protested in Chesterfield, they tended to recall an era of stronger unions and less inequality, but not look forward to a different society altogether. It is almost inevitable that resistance movements will do this, because we make use of familiar reference points in our history to make sense of today.

But we need to be conscious of how even the way we "frame the debate" might involve the subtle acceptance of capitalism, because it is difficult to imagine our lives without markets. The ability of capitalism to develop these relations in such a way as they appear "natural" is a key source of its social power, without which it could not sustain itself as a system.

If we move down a few steps in the ladder – from broad generalisations about capitalism to more historically specific phases of its existence – we can see how certain ideas come to crystallize across decades as a *zeitgeist*: 'a spirit of the age'. Until very recently, our own age was marked by a dramatic intensification of the naturalizing tendencies of capitalism: few even mentioned it by name such was its apparent indestructibility. It was just accepted as the "way of things are", as the march of capital with its unprecedented expansion across the globe, and into every single aspect of our lives, would go on and on. Gordon Brown thought he had overcome "boom and bust" and he was not alone - most economists and politicians thought that globalisation offered a virtuous circle of market-led growth and prosperity.

Politics in an age of realism

The idea of a paradigm of 'capitalist realism' points to some of the most important debates on the post-war left about the future of capitalism and its remarkable power of endurance. This principally comes back to the "Marcuse problematic", named after the German Marxist who became a darling of the 1968 New Left in the United States. It is the question of whether capitalism in its current stage has evolved ever-more sophisticated coping strategies that are routinely successful in managing class contradiction through a dual process of absorption, and the outright political defeat of resistance movements.

Marcuse's original point was that, while Marx correctly analysed the class contradictions of capitalism, his expectation that with greater misery would come greater political radicalisation was wrong. The problem was that in advanced capitalist countries the working class had become increasingly incorporated into the system: trade union and labour practices had tied workers institutionally to their bosses and the state, the expansion of consumerism had intensified dependency on the market and created false needs and wants. The result was a cultural condition in which capitalist hegemony was largely accepted.

In *One Dimensional Man*, Marcuse developed his analysis of the evolution of capitalist alienation with the advent of consumer society in the West. This had seen a transformation in the form of alienation, which was not merely expressed in an alienated detachment from the products of labour, but also conversely the tendency to see commodities as the source of our humanity. As he put it, "the people recognize themselves in their commodities; they find their soul in their automobile, hi-fi set, split-level home, kitchen equipment."[23] This inevitably undermined the class-consciousness of workers, who would increasingly see themselves as consumers, implicitly identifying self-improvement with the accumulation of things.

However, in this period Marcuse tended to over-emphasise the stability of consumer society and he spent much of the last part of his life, after the radicalisation of '68, trying to correct the pessimism of his writings in the early 1960s. Nonetheless, the transition from the Fordist social model to the post-Fordist paradigm of neoliberalism in the 1980s further intensified many of the tendencies lodged within the consumer society that Marcuse had originally identified. With the collapse of the Soviet Union these processes globalised and brought about the age of capitalist realism as hope in an alternative to the system faded starkly from view.

Both Mark Fisher and the philosopher Slavoj Žižek consider the film *Children of Men* as a brilliant analogy for the capitalist realist paradigm. The plot device at the core of the film (that humanity has become infertile and no more babies are being born anywhere in the world) is a metaphor for something else: what if there is no future? In a new interpretation of Marx's "force is the midwife of a new society",[24] it becomes, in this sense, re-posed as, "what if there are no more midwives – if there is no revolution only a slow decline into environmental and social collapse?" The film is thus permeated by a sense of despair and bleakness as humanity stands at its nadir with no apparent way out. Religious sects emerge; resistance takes the form of terrorism and 'propaganda of the deed' actions. Much of the world is lawless, racism and nationalism are rampant, and Britain survives but only through totalitarianism as the basis of its "civilization". The film's power lies in the eerie familiarity of the narrative it depicts. The experiences of the film – concentration camps, warlords, genocide, etc. – are instantly recognisable to us, not of course in their totality, but as isolated moments common to our contemporary existence. Indeed, as an imagined totality the familiarity of the film serves to underline Frederic Jameson's famous point that it has become "easier for us to imagine the end of the world than the end of capitalism".[25] This is the central paradox of capitalist realism: the juxtaposition between the continued injustice and crises of capital and the apparent passing away of the opportunity to transcend it. The film speaks to the challenge for anticapitalists politics when hope appears to have been lost. It follows Theo Faron, a civil servant, once politically active, now cynical and apathetic, as he is forced to negotiate terroristic resistance movements and a totalitarian government. In one scene, his earlier hopes for progressive social change are recalled through photos of him and his family, with Stop the War placards on the anti-Iraq war marches. In this way, the film promotes the idea that the decline of the left as a social power runs parallel to the social decline of society itself. A society without a strong left is, thus, a society without a conscience or future.

Other cultural references confirm Jameson's point – the difficulty in imagining alternatives to capitalism – from the opposite angle by portraying as distant and farfetched economic systems that are organised on the basis of collectivism and human need. A subplot in one episode of *Star Trek; the Next Generation* (The Neutral Zone) sees the crew discover a piece of apparent space debris from 21st century earth, only to discover it contains cryogenically frozen bodies.

Brought back to life on the Enterprise, an American businessman asks pugnaciously to be taken to his accountant on earth to see how his stocks are doing only to be told, that "society is no longer obsessed by the accumulation of things, want and scarcity have been abolished". Bewildered the 21st century Earthling, asks "what's the point then?", to which the crew responds that self-improvement and collective humanity have become the meaning of life, and he should "just enjoy it". In this world of self-betterment, science and discovery, the old habits of our century – its drudgery, exploitation and profiteering – appear to the Enterprise crew as anachronisms. For us, however, the rational economic system of Star Trek appears farfetched, if not impossible. It is a stark contrast from the familiarity of the doom portrayed in *Children of Men*. If one point of connection exists between these two narratives, it is when one of the Enterprise crew asks, "it makes you wonder how our species survived the 21st century?"[26]

The idea of capitalist realism is not that there is *no* resistance. Capitalism always provokes it – the exploitation of labour by capital will always give rises to struggles over the unequal distribution of wealth intrinsic to this process. Neither is the argument that the working class has lost all sense of its class consciousness or notions of collective solidarity and social power. Working class communities and organisations keep alive these ideas and cultural practices, while the unequal distribution of wealth provides a material basis for a sense of class injustice – like the simple fact that bankers are getting bailed out, while the great majority are seeing job losses, wage cuts and benefits reduced. Capitalist realism is simply a way of talking about the widespread belief that there is no *alternative* to capitalism. All we can hope for are mild reforms to tame the savage beast.

Past defeats of workers' organisations have contributed to a restructuring of capitalism that has increased inequality and fragmentation within the working class, and undermined its ability to resist further attacks. This has intersected with a decline in its political radicalisation, specifically a decline in its hope and aspiration for a fundamentally different system, as socialism was discredited by the experience of Stalinism in the 20th century. These factors are certainly not *absolute* determinisms. The ebbs and flows of resistance still continue. We know that there are many millions of people around the world who still identify as socialists or communists (even if their understanding of this has been influenced by the advent of neoliberalism, coupled with the expansion of capitalism in states such as China and India). In the western world, which was seen as the victorious side in the Cold War that shaped the history of the last century, the effect of these changes on the left has been significant. Nothing will be gained from a radical perspective that attempts to deny the enormity of these changes – we have to understand these processes in order to develop the politics that can overcome the profound challenges faced by 21st century socialists.

The default role for the great mass of people in advanced capitalism is increasingly the consumer-spectator.[27] The spectacle of the reality show TV, rampant consumerism which confronts the disempowered political individual looking at an increasingly precarious economic future, are the *Leitmotif* of modern life in much of the West. We can often be propelled into action against an outrageous injustice, but it is difficult to translate this into serious long term opposition to the system. Often, the dominant attitude can be cynicism. The expenses scandal in Britain was largely met with a resigned sense of recognition – the "we already knew they were corrupt" outlook. While it's undoubtedly a good thing that corruption stands exposed, we need to be aware that the way this can be internalised into the minds of large numbers of ordinary people is to reinforce their alienation from politics.

One interesting feature of this situation is how capitalist realism also frames the terms for resistance to the system. The resistance to austerity and dictators in the Arab Spring has often been dominated by the demands for citizenship, individual rights and for more democracy: in short, for more control over our lives. In the student rebellion in Britain last year, a central point of antagonism was the democratic deficit: that the Liberal Democrats had won the support of millions of young people due to their policy on free higher education, but in less than six months of being in government had supported fees of £9,000 per year. This movement was about a class-based injustice, but the language of class resistance was not as prominent as would have been expected in earlier decades.

Similarly, the March for the Alternative demonstration led by the TUC in spring 2011 had an overt-class dynamic – it was joined by huge contingents of low paid public sector workers being hurt by austerity – but in its "pitch", its dominant narrative from the top echelons of the platform, speakers recalled the great marches for democratic rights and social justice in the 20th century rather than the language of working class resistance. This is not a criticism so much as an observation. Today, mass movements will often organise large strata of concerned, indeed outraged ("*indignados*"), citizens, who value the individual freedoms that they have won, that draw on a liberal value system, but who share a common sense of injustice with attack after attack hitting the rights and gains of working people. So the class aspect can be only implicit rather than overt and radical liberal ideas have often been more prominent than socialist ones.

The confidence of the bourgeoisie in their own system was best expressed in the Fukuyama thesis[28], which claimed that with the collapse of the Soviet Union we had arrived at the end of history: there was now no alternative to liberal capitalism. Whilst Marx argued that communism would be the end of history (though he also referred to it as the beginning of a new history – simply the end of systems of social oppression), Fukuyama, perhaps truer to Hegel's original teleology[29], argued that the end of history had been ushered in by the fall of the Soviet Union and the triumph of the West. A political system that was increasingly narrow in its ideological variations, liberalism, had won out. Indeed, the constitutional liberalism of the American Revolution had trumped the class conflicts of the French and Russian 'models'. In short, it was liberalism and not communism that had monopolised modernity. Inevitably, the radical left largely rejected this thesis.[30]

Indeed, the left had to if it was to maintain any relevance. Instead it tended to emphasise was the episodic nature of the liberal moment in the early 90s, the temporary and partial setbacks for the left, or even, with the fall of the Soviet Union, a chance to forge a new left unencumbered by Stalinism. True as this was, in practice the left suffered a certain intellectual paralysis in the face of the Fukuyama challenge. Žižek argued that the radical left only formally rejected the thesis while actually absorbing many of its central assumptions. The "Fukuyama taboo" on the left meant for Žižek that, in "a way we all were until now Fukuyama-ists. Even radical leftists were not thinking about what can replace capitalism... they were demanding more social justice, more rights for women, and so on, from within the system."[31] Žižek makes a powerful case that cuts across not only the liberal consensus of wider society, but also the dominant assumptions of the radical left. The idea that history has decided on liberal democratic capitalism, that it is simply taboo, "not the done thing", to challenge it, and that this finds its reflection on the limited and partial demands that the radical left seeks to popularise, speaks to many of the problems of modern day Marxism. In a sense, despite the claims of the revolutionary left, Eduard Bernstein's perspective of slow gradual change to the system won out - even if actual social democratic reformism seems to be in decline.

Žižek makes the point that capitalism is a remarkably elastic system. Take, for example, how it has absorbed some of the most radical resistance currents of the post-1968 epoch. It was able to incorporate many of the demands of movements that promoted new forms of identity politics, at least for long enough to demobilise and fragment them, often on class lines (the divisions, for example, between the myriad forms of feminism in the 1980s and 90s testify to this). This elasticity gave capitalism a lasting power in the face of the new left movements of the 60s and 70s. The kind of immediate demands that were popularised – ending the war in Vietnam or achieving equality in the eyes of the law – were such that success in these quarters, no matter how important, did not bring into question the capitalist system. Again, this is not a criticism designed to stand aloof from the tremendous radical legacy left behind by these social movements. Neither are we saying that we should not organise mass movements around the immediate concerns of working people, women and ethnic minorities – we must continue to do this – but simply to recognise their partiality, their limitations, if radical politics is to actually seek to move beyond capitalism itself.

The problems of capitalist realism are not simply part of the lament of listless leftist intellectuals who feel that there is no clear way forward for a declining movement. Workers experience this feeling too. This might take the form of living and working in communities that still feel they have lost the power they once had over capital. But they might also feel the effects of the individualisation that neoliberalism has fostered. With the decline of collective social organisations (like the unions) and expansion of flexible labour markets, insecurity and inequality within the working class has fostered a politics of social mobility that has so far trumped the traditional politics of class struggle.[32] We will come onto the way that the new realism has affected working class organisation in the following chapters.

In Goethe's Faust, the devil Mephistopheles introduces himself by saying "I am the spirit of perpetual negation".[33] This could be considered an apt description for the left today, bereft of a working example where they hold power and can demonstrate in practice that they can offer a credible alternative to capitalism. It leaves the left as minority, agitators, "trouble-makers", or "wreckers" as Tony Blair once put it.[34] Of course, in a world of hypocrisy and spin-doctored reaction, we can be proud to be "wreckers" of the corporations' plans, but it poses the problem of power and credibility. In an era characterised by constant movement, the danger for the left is to be seen as resistant to change and harking back to bygone eras. If the political right veil their arguments, however hypocritically, in the ideals of progress, change and modernisation, they can appeal to a sense of frustration with the status quo – and take advantage again of our uncertain sense of time; that leaves our aspirations about the future open to political manipulation. It also means that the left can appear as the conservative "immobilisers" of change.[35] Already at a disadvantage in how wider society perceives the arguments of the radical left, if we are seen as dinosaurs obstructing change, then the right can all too easily capture the zeitgeist. In the dominant narrative of the Anglo-Saxon political elite, the unions are the classical immobilisers, attempting to arrest the changes being wrought by capitalism. Unions are presented as defending the sectional interests of organised labour against the mass of the electorate, and trying half-heartedly to stop the neoliberal juggernaut before succumbing to the new realism.

The radical left too has tended to ape the larger working class organisations. "Save the NHS", "no to cuts" are popular, and indeed necessary, slogans - but they are inevitably limited. They don't point to an alternative and cannot capture the spirit of progress, modernisation, even "revolution", which is often co-opted by the centre right. So, the challenge we face today can be summarised as the need to build political organisations that appeal to the "spirit of the new", that reclaim the idea of progress, promote resistance that makes incursion on the power of capital and also have credibility in the eyes of large numbers of working people.

This can overcome a central problem that the radical left has lost its claim to represent the heirs to the radical Enlightenment tradition in Western modernity; with its ideal that human society can be rationally organised and successively transformed through progressive social and technical changes. Now it is co-opted by the neoliberal centre ground who have dishonestly cloaked a reactionary political agenda, such as NHS privatisation dressed up as "reform", in the language of modernisation. But, this is not merely about deliberately misleading ideological claims, it is also because capitalism continually succeeds in realising technological, spatial and aesthetic transformations. From the communications revolution, to the transformation of urban life through neoliberal regeneration programmes, and continual change in cultural forms of life, these processes foster a sense of progress and renewal, even though their realisation has a "darker side" involving widespread impoverishment and growing social inequality. The result is that, in comparison, socialist politics can appear to be looking backwards to the past; a hopeless attempt to revive a dead social experiment, which in the minds of many people, suffered a decisive defeat. This problem will not be solved easily, but when it is, we can be sure it will involve having to think about the kind of language we use to revive our agenda; about how the audience perceives it; about how our practices and organisational forms will need to change in order to render ourselves attractive and modern, in "the spirit of the age", just as much as getting the politics right.

So, what ushered in the age of capitalist realism? It is impossible to pinpoint an exact moment, but there is a convergence of factors which led to the ascendancy of capital over all works of life. Countries like Britain were faced with a stark choice in the 1970s, as the Fordist model went into crisis. Revivify and radicalise working class organisations to undertake a new assault on capitalist power, or face an almighty offensive and neoliberal transformation. Political failures on the part of the left and the union tops – which represented in an important sense a failure to realise the stakes involved in the struggle, a complacency that gains would be defended without mass, generalised resistance - intersected with a growth in the political hegemony of Neoliberalism. Individualist politics of social mobility were triumphant over those of class struggle. A cultural reality underpinned by structural economic changes that boosted inequality inside the working and middle classes. The collapse of so-called "actually existing socialism", as Stalinist ideologues once called it, also seemed to confirm that the struggle for communism was a failed social experiment, not a new phase of human society. In any case, real, living socialist transformation was a million miles from the "actually existing" Soviet systems. Socialism, in this sense, had *already been* badly undermined. For although it guaranteed work and social provision, for many, inside and outside these states, it seemed to be as alienating as capitalism and worse insofar as it had a fascistic state along with the dreary sameness of its culture and everyday life. As the Polish saying of the 1980s cynically put it, "under capitalism man exploits man; under socialism *the reverse is true*".

The reply to the theorists of capitalist realism is simple enough: this is all well and good as a description of 1991-2008, but it is hopeless as a description of the post Lehman Brothers world. This is one of the conclusions that Paul Mason has come to in his new book *Why It's Kicking Off Everywhere; the New Global Revolutions,* where he has argued that the revolts and revolutions of 2008 – 2011 signalled, "the age of capitalist realism was over".[36]

Naturally, whether you agree with this hinges on what precisely you mean by capitalist realism. Mason's evocative literary portrait of the new resistance brings to life the transformation in consciousness we have seen since 2008. A space has opened up for critical evaluation of capitalism and how it might be transcended. We would show greater caution as to the extent to which this has actually, substantively, undermined capitalist realism. At the moment, we have not yet seen the revivification of a coherent alternative to capitalism.

This problem leads us back to the crisis of Marxism. It has lost its hegemony as the "natural" emancipatory project for people that want to change the world. And this means, as Mason readily admits, that there is "no ideology driving [the new] movement and no coherent vision of an alternative society".[37] Instead, the new movements give rise to an ensemble of ideas and influences, though marked by a radical anticapitalist streak, and largely favouring horizontal methods of organising over the hierarchies of the 'old left'. With the displacement of Marxism there is a relative absence of real strategy, i.e. a relative lack of discussion around how political power should be used, and around what form and organisation a challenge for power should take, if we are to win radical change. While talking about political power might appear far removed from the current stage of resistance, unless we do so, then we are implicitly reinforcing the capitalist realist logic of the current moment.

In light of both the problem of capitalist realism and the

emerging opportunity to challenge it, Žižek and Badiou have embarked on an intellectual project summed up by "the idea of communism".[38] Žižek co-organised a conference in London in 2009 to discuss this challenge - can we get the idea of a post-capitalist working class state back into the mainstream? Can we rescue communism from the failed and barbaric legacy of Stalinism? The fact these questions are even being debated again points to a much brighter future for the radical left.

Indeed, we need to think creatively about what Marxism means today. We can't fall into the trap of harking back to the past era, but have to render our politics thoroughly modern. In the same vein, it will be one thing to win a generation of radical activists to revivified Marxist politics – and this may well be an initial stage already underway – but beyond this, the far greater challenge is to establish a new socialist hegemony in the working class movement.

In Britain, the working class has historically been thoroughly imbued with a reformist, semi liberal spirit of "gradualism reformism" backed up by powerful trade unions. This all changed during and after the 1980s to be replaced by a new reality of declining union membership, a dramatic move to the right by many on the left, the end of the 'gradualist' agenda and the dawn of the monstrosity of New Labour. It's to the legacy of this politics we shall now turn.

New Labour globalised

Global capitalism can be cruel in its symbolism. A tale of two buildings speaks to a wider set of transformations in working class politics. The Communist Party of Great Britain, once numbering 50,000 members after the Second World War, was at the centre of the British labour movement before it split in 1991. Its old headquarters, at 16 King Street in Covent Garden, is today a branch of HSBC, one of the biggest banks in the world. The miners' union, the NUM, undertook one of the greatest of battles against the Thatcher government in 1984 – '85, a decisive moment for these workers, as they were rightly seen as the advanced guard of the British labour movement. Their defeat made possible post-industrial Britain. In December 2011, it was announced that Sheffield council was granting permission for the old NUM headquarters, the very nerve centre of the miners' strike, to be turned into a casino.

Nowhere is this shift to the right better illustrated than in the changing nature of the Labour Party and how it defined mainstream working class politics in Britain. Indeed, no discussion on the fate and future of the working class and socialist politics in Britain is complete without a clear under-standing of where the Labour Party fits in. And it is often a contradictory state of affairs. Whilst many joined Labour after 2010 to oppose the Tories' cuts, by New Years 2012 Ed Balls and Ed Miliband were doing their best to drive them out again, by accepting the logic of the Coalition cuts, and agreeing that they would not reverse any cuts once in power. Today, most people shrug when a Labour leader delivers yet another pro-market, pro-business, "outburst", but how exactly did it get to this bad?

Anthony Giddens, a British sociologist and intellectual heavyweight in the original Blairite project, which was euphemistically termed the "Third Way", summed up the basis of the new, realist way of thinking, as it was understood by the Labour Party leadership:

No one has any alternatives to capitalism; the arguments that remain concern how far and in what ways capitalism should be governed and regulated.[39]

This attitude was the bedrock of what became New Labour. A transformation which has been referred justly to as "Thatcher's greatest victory", for it represented a capitulation to the neoliberal political agenda she had pioneered in the 1980s. "New Labour, New Britain" was the slogan of the 1995 conference. It was a bold and nationalistic image designed to capture the spirit of the new, so-called "cool Britannia" ethos of the 1990s. It would mark the opening of a radically different era in the history of the Labour Party, no longer as a party of labour in the traditional sense, but a party that could embrace "middle England" (along with media moguls, retailers and industrialists) and become a trusted, even favoured, party of British capitalism during the hey days of the globalisation boom.

The significance of Giddens' statement lies in how the Labour Party had previously understood its project. The idea of "gradualism" presupposed, in theory at least, a steady and evolving transformation away from societies dominated by markets, and towards public ownership and democratic control. In an important sense, it was never *overtly pro-capitalist* in its message, even though, once in power, Labour sought to integrate the unions into the management of the "national interest" in order to strengthen British industrial capital and improve its global competitiveness. The left turn of the early 1980s around Tony Benn's vision of democratic socialism, which succeeded in winning the party to a series of more radical policies on nationalisation, workplace democracy and democratisation, promised a series of dramatic reforms "within weeks" of taking power.[40] But this was exceptionally radical in Labour's wider history and even then, in its totality, the manifesto was ultimately committed to strengthening the public aspect of a mixed capitalist economy. Crucially however, it was articulated and promoted by Tony Benn, not the centrist party leadership around Michael Foot, as a set of fundamental socialist measures, as a genuine alternative to capitalism. This expressed the simple fact that the early 1980s were a time when such measures were being talked about as tangible aspirations of government policy.

Giddens' statement, which tellingly parroted Thatcher's dictum "there is no alternative", thus brutally encapsulated how the left was ultimately defeated within the party, and how capitalist realism had been brought well and truly into the working class movement. It was this that arguably gave New Labour its distinctive, special role in the political defeat of the labour movement. For, whereas Thatcher had presented a stark antagonism – a point of visceral hatred and opposition for millions of trade unionists – the Blair project sought to establish a new hegemony around a broadly similar agenda *inside* the working class. This would certainly create a new antagonism between Labour and its traditional supporters, but it also served to compound feelings of alienation, defeat and weakness amongst this base. In this very important sense (by dismantling a mass pole of opposition to neoliberalism that was based on the working class movement) it was arguably a far more serious defeat than those brought about by the brute force and power of the Thatcher offensive. A new consensus was established around her legacy, with Labour under Blair taking the project of pro-market restructuring far further into the public sector than the Tories had dared to.

In a fashion typical of the neoliberal revolution, New Labour laid claim to the discourse of modernisation and forward renewal. In fact, it did so far more confidently and assertively than traditional Thatcherism had, or could do. For the latter always sought to integrate its classical liberalism with traditional Tory values, such as its patriarchal attitudes to family life. In contrast, New Labour was much more overt and consistent in its liberalism: the Cool Britannia ethos invoked a trendy and progressive capitalism that reached out to the cosmopolitan entrepreneurial generation, alienated from old school Conservatism. This was a capitalism in which affluent sections of women, ethnic minorities and the gay community could identify with confidently, in a way they often could not with the Tories. Its notion of the modern simply corresponded to the raw power of capitalism and so "being modern" meant adapting to its demands and impulses.[41] Indeed, New Labour was about capitalist realism in a way that Thatcherism-proper could never quite be. The latter defined itself in opposition to the so-called "enemy within" of the socialist labour movement, but New Labour simply defined itself in opposition to what was "old". This actually encompassed class politics "from below", in the form of working class resistance to capitalism, and "from above", in the form of the offensive of the Thatcher years. New Labour broke with the politics of class by denying its operative existence as a meaningful cleavage in the new times.

There was in fact something distinctively *post*modern about its attempt to discursively break free from the old dichotomies of class. By denying the existence of the antagonistic relationship between the rich and poor – by insisting the mere mention of it was the "old" politics, New Labour discourse evaded the need to give a positive statement of its trenchant commitment to global capitalism and the entrepreneurial society. It was as if "no such generalization were possible". [42] Its historical distinctiveness, even when put in contrast to the rightward shift of social democratic parties across Europe in the globalisation years, was that it largely abandoned the discourse of class compromise. The measures proposed for greater liberalisation of markets and privatisation were, it was claimed, in the *general interest* of all. The notion of socialism had to be completely recast to make this possible. The removal of Clause 4 of the party constitution symbolised the transition between "new" and "old" Labour. In the fashion of being all things to all people, the New Labour Clause 4 read: "for each of us the means to realise our true potential and for all of us a community in which power, wealth and opportunity are in the hands of the many not the few, where the rights we enjoy reflect the duties we owe, and where we live together, freely, in a spirit of solidarity, tolerance and respect". Traditionally, in consonance with the politics of "gradualism", Labour had ultimately been committed to achieving democratic control of the means of production and exchange. The removal of this aspiration was unimportant in terms of its practical policy, for Labour had never made any serious attempt to realise the final goal. It was indicative of a dramatic change in culture, not just in the Labour Party, but across society. The opposition to the removal of Clause 4 in 1995 was muted, tokenistic and eventually forgotten.[43] This was a discourse that New Labour would utilise throughout its time in office, precisely in order to camouflage the fact they saw market forces as essential in realising "tolerance" and "solidarity". For Blair, insofar as socialism had any operative impact on his ideological moorings, it was recast as a merely ethical state of being, a vague commitment to unspecified notions of social justice.

Inevitably this kind of outlook fed into the loss of meaning in politics. Indeed, this is another feature of capitalist realism, which owes much to the New Labour experience. In this new era, elections can be won on "values", inevitably vague and amorphous, for there is little difference on policy between the competing sides. It makes perfect sense that this would happen once mainstream politics converged around a neoliberal centre ground. In the absence of sharp ideological conflicts, but with the continued existence of multi-party system, arguments will remain fierce in tone despite substantial agreement existing on policy. New Labour were truly artful when it came to the political euphemism. Privatisation was translated into reform and modernisation; labour market insecurity likewise was termed flexibility; the invasion of sovereign states was labelled 'regime change' or 'humanitarian intervention', and the expansion of capitalism globally was called 'trade and financial liberalisation'. New Labour did not invent all these terms, but they were expert at using them. During their years in office, talking about capitalism was largely a preserve of anti-globalisation protestors, and even then only the more radical wing of the movement.

They succeeded in pushing the Tories rightwards onto issues their traditional supporters favoured, but left the wider electorate alienated, particularly on Europe. It was only with the rebranding exercise under David Cameron that the Tories learnt to play by the rules of New Labour and started to appeal to "progressive values" to legitimise their right-wing agenda.

The crux of the loss of meaning in British politics, then, is how a discourse more commonly associated with social liberalism came to be used to legitimise the "tough" classical liberalism and authoritarian conservatism of the Thatcher decade. This was not merely a question of economic policy. New Labour's offensive on civil liberties, the rights of asylum seekers, and anti-social behaviour, or even the dramatic expansion of police numbers under the principle of being tough on crime, not to mention their foreign policy, all stood, rationally speaking, in the tradition of authoritarian and hawkish conservatism. But in their language Labour drew on the vocabulary of progressive policies, fairness, justice, and so on. Even the term "radical" was transmogrified into a measure of how far to the right Labour could move. As Stuart Hall observed this left opponents of New Labour with a real linguistic problem:

The very idea of the 'social' and the 'public' has been specifically liquidated by New Labour. It has been New Labour's historic project to end the notion of the social as you and I understand it... But what makes it complicated is that there are plenty of references in New Labour to building up community. They have bought the language and evacuated it. You ask me about progressive politics. Progressive politics is in their mouth every day. Community is in their mouth every day. Reform has been absorbed by them and re-used in quite a different way. It's that transvaluation of all the key terms, that linguistic move that New Labour has made, which presents anyone who is trying to take a critical approach with a tremendous problem. What terms can you use to speak about your objections?[44]

It would be wrong to blame it all this on Tony Blair. Labour undertook a long march rightwards many years previously, after the height of its radicalism in 1980 – 1983. Under Neil Kinnock, ironically once thought of as a leftist in Labour Party terms, a bitter struggle was waged against the radical wing of the party. The campaign included purging left radical Labour militants, destroying its grassroots democracy and negating any possibility of Labour putting forward a fundamental alternative to Thatcherism. The Policy Review of 1987 – 89 dumped key pillars of their programme, indeed of the post-war consensus, as it had existed before 1979. Their electoral slogan of 1992, "to restore a consensus" in British politics was apt, but not as they intended, for the party had increasingly fallen behind the new, Thatcherite unanimity.

The strategy pursued by Blair, Peter Mandelson and the other New Labour ideologues was consciously imported from the Democrats in the US. It was the policy of Triangulation, originally developed by Democrat strategist Dick Morris.[45] Triangulation is the perfect strategy for an apparently post-ideological age, for it is neither explicitly "left or right", but instead purports to be deeply pragmatic and technocratic. It takes the neoliberal centre ground as the "common sense" terrain of modern politics. It then seeks to actively build alliances amongst social groups, often with mutually antagonistic interests on the left and the right, to integrate them into this political consensus. The point was to make social groups, like the unions, appear to have been listened to, their concerns registered, perhaps some of the less controversial policies even accepted, but never to promise too much.

In Britain, New Labour pioneered a specific form of triangulation at the level of practical policy by boosting welfare spending, expanding the size of the public sector. Yet, in the process of doing so, they gave unprecedented opportunities to private business to make money. The Private Finance Initiative, for example, where the private sector would fund capital investment and then lease hospitals and schools back to the state, cost £20 billion more than if the original outlay had simply been funded by the state. The railways, though privatised under the Tories, were kept that way by Labour, while the annual costs of subsidising the profit-making franchises quintupled to £5 billion by 2011.[46] The City Academies programme allowed private firms, religious groups or individuals to contribute up to £2 million to set up a school they would have complete control over, even though the government would stump up as much as £35 million to open it.[47] We could go on. Examples of how state expenditure became quite tailored to the needs of private capital are numerous. New Labour thus influenced and nurtured neoliberalism as the "project of class power", as Harvey so appropriately labelled it. For this kind of systematic use of public investment to help open up opportunities for private capital has become an essential part of how big business has sought to direct the political agenda. David Cameron's government may be reversing much of the increased public expenditure of the New Labour years in their austerity programme, but they have dramatically extended the same privatisation agenda. Indeed, today's government health and education reforms are opening up huge financial opportunities for the private sector that, due to their vast scale, dwarf the more limited programmes of the Blair government.

The rise and consolidation of New Labour cannot be seen outside of the dramatic global changes of the post-1989 world. Labour in power gave a political expression to a series of contextual, cultural and economic shifts. One was the dramatic capitalist internationalisation of these years, the creation of a 'global neoliberal village', that fostered a superficially cosmopolitan air, but which apparently progressive ethos disguised a darker undercurrent of sweatshops. Another change was the growth of anti-migrant racism, rising global inequality, and a "war on terror" without apparent end. It was, though, the economic and institutional integration of this period around the neoliberal consensus that made possible the globalisation of the politics of New Labour. With the British and American economies promoting the idea that neoliberalisation the normal pressures of the business cycle, the pressure on other economies (and specifically other social democratic parties in Europe) to follow this example in order to compete was considerable. Across the European Union, New Labour put itself in the advance guard of internationalising the new ethos of capitalist realism. The Lisbon Agenda, the Bologna Process, the Agenda 2010 programme of the German social democracy, the Treaty of Lisbon, are all examples of how New Labour influenced wider European politics.

The relative historical novelty of New Labour-proper remained, however, its capacity for doublespeak: its ability to present, apparently without irony, aggressively anti-working class policies as in the interests of *all*. This, however, could never be quite fully absorbed by the other parties of European social democracy. For them, like Gerhard Schröder's *Neue Mitte* for example, it was far more convincing to package up neoliberalism in the "old" language of class compromise as necessary concessions to the new realities of the globalised order.

As a global force, social democracy stood, nonetheless, quite consistently at the centre of the web of connections that tied together the neoliberal order. It was, and remains, interwoven through a thousand personal and political ties into the fabric of the international system. A short list of a few individuals will illustrate their role. Neil Kinnock went onto become a European Commissioner, his wife became a Labour MEP. His son Stephen, meanwhile, is the director of the World Economic Forum (WEF), while the latter's wife became Denmark's first ever female prime minister. One of the architects of New Labour, Peter Mandelson, became the Trade Commissioner in the EU during the Doha Round. Pascal Lamy, the Director General of the World Trade Organisation (WTO), is a longstanding member of the French Socialist Party. Dominique Strauss Kahn, infamous for his alleged sexual assault of a maid at a New York hotel, was (until his disgrace) the president of the International Monetary Fund (IMF) and was another leading figure of the French Socialists. Had it not been for the scandal he would almost certainly have been the party's next presidential candidate. The position of these figures within the establishment and their politics are almost identical to Italy's Romano Prodi, twice Italian prime minister and one-time head of the European Commission.

Although Prodi was never a member of a social democratic party, he twice headed centre-left coalitions and he encapsulates the kind of "progressive" neoliberalism that today dominates much of the European political scene. It is these figures and people like them that have shaped the response of social democracy to the current economic crisis. Furthermore, quite naturally given their relationship to the process of globalisation, they have helped foster a new political consensus based upon a dramatic socialisation of private financial losses and parallel bailouts of debtor nations. This was continuity-neoliberalism in the Harvey sense of the term It was continuity with the project of "class power" that used the state to defend the investments of financialized capital. In short, while the economic sustainability of these measures is highly doubtful, their class basis is not.

Labour 'after New Labour' follows the same pattern, but we can see in microcosm how its leaders have sought to re-orientate the party in a political context where there is widespread popular hostility towards financial institutions, but without dramatically changing policy. The 2010 leadership election remarkably saw two brothers – sons of the late Marxist Ralph Miliband, but very far removed from him politically – dominate the contest. Ed was the candidate of the moderate union leaders and centre-left of the party, while David was the continuity New Labour candidate. Ed Miliband won, but only thanks to trade union votes – reflecting just how far the grassroots of the party membership had moved to the right over the years. The fact that most of them backed the man widely seen as Blair's candidate, given the wider public mood of hostility towards New Labour, was remarkable. Ed Miliband at least recognised there had to be some kind of shift in how the party was perceived, even though there was no question of a radical move to the left in its policy. He drew on electoral statistics during his campaign that showed Labour had to win back largely working class, blue collar sections of the electorate to recoup the 5 million votes it lost since 1997.[48] Under his leadership the strategy can be summed up as often ill-conceived attempts at real politic populism. Rhetorically he has targeted the banks for much criticism and called for an end to "crony capitalism", without substantively disagreeing with the political consensus around the financial bailsouts. He won support for a few timely interventions during the phone hacking crisis, as David Cameron's relationship with Andy Coulson mired him in the scandal. But his populism, based on the idea of the "squeezed middle", has also extended to caving in on government attacks on the poorest – refusing, for example, to join the House of Lords clergy in condemning the cap on benefit claimants. He also wrote an introduction to the Blue Labour manifesto, a conservative (with a small c) movement in the party that harked back to the community populism of Ramsay Macdonald. Its critique cut across "old", "centralizing" Labour, and the "new", City of London Labour. But its attack on "old" Labour counter-posed the state sector to the traditional working class community, and thus it parroted much of Cameron's "big society" hypocrisy in a time of cuts. But Maurice Glasman, the main Blue Labour ideologue, was later discredited when he argued Labour needed to reach out to those who supported the English Defence League[49], leaving Miliband floundering.

It is however in his attitude to the resistance to the cuts that the limitations of Miliband's populism can be most clearly seen. He took a conscious decision not march with the 500,000 trade unionists on TUC demonstration, even though he encouraged his shadow cabinet to do so, and even though he did address the rally at the end. It was a conscious move to create a kind of "presidential", triangulation feel around his self-image: he was not *of the marchers*, but he would *speak to the marchers*. It was a subtlety that was quite deliberate; he didn't want to be associated with active resistance to the cuts, for fear it would damage his respectability. But he did want to be seen "to listen" in order to win the votes of those fighting. The same outlook led him to say of the Occupy movement, that it had "challenged politics", but he did not go down to actually speak to the protesters' real concerns. He similarly refused to respond when the BBC attempted to set up interviews with student leaders in the movement of 2010. It might appear clever, but just like Kinnock (who took a similar attitude to the extra parliamentary resistance to Thatcher in the 1980s – careful to not outright oppose, but careful not to get involved, and doing his best to call it off wherever possible) the result are losses of support on both the right and the left. For the right he is '"red"' just for listening, for the left he is a traitor for not supporting.

Indeed, two key moments undermined all other attempts Miliband made to "listen" to the movement. First, he went outright opposed the pension strikes in June 2011 of civil servants, teachers and lecturers. Later, when the larger strike in November came, he would make noises of sympathy without offering categorical support. For the strikers this was at best inadequate, if not an outright betrayal. Second, he declared Labour's support for the public sector pay freeze and said they would not promise to reverse the Tory cuts. Somewhat unsurprisingly, by the end of January 2012, the Tories were again riding high on the opinion polls. It is a classic lesson for the electoral opportunist to not to live and die by public opinion, for Miliband's populism was in a certain sense rational for an opportunist. It was based on the fact that most people do not support most strikes, while most people also think that some cuts are necessary. But these were not normal strikes – literally millions took action – and the result was a wave of public support. Similarly, failing to commit to undoing the damage of the Tory cuts undermined their claim to have an alternative at all. After all, the natural reaction of the electorate should be obvious to the Labour leaders: "if they aren't going to undo the damage, then what's the point?" Moreover, the only times Miliband made specific policies it was clear the "alternative" wasn't radically different. He promised, for example, to reduce fees for higher education from £9,000 to £6,000 – but this was a gesture so minimal, it could hardly claim to represent an alternative policy, let alone a "new capitalism".

Ed Miliband as an individual is certainly not the problem. Rather, he is indicative of a deeper and far reaching transformation that has taken place in the heart of the Labour Party. It is this extensive set of changes that was expressed by a majority of its members backing a pro-Blair, pro-Iraq war candidate in its

2010 leadership election. It has changed the class outlook of large sections of the wider party and especially the parliamentary tops. This can be seen clearly when one looks at Progress, a Blairite think thank at the heart of New Labour. It has generated nearly £3 million in donations in the last few years, with Lord Sainsbury alone donating £250,000. In early 2011 Progress put on a day event funded by Vodafone, Sky and Bell Pottinger, an international PR firm which was co-founded by Lord Bell, Thatcher's media adviser when she was Prime Minister.[50] While the social democracy in Germany used to be considered "a state within a state", Progress is widely considered a "party within a party".[51]

Meanwhile, the Labour Party as a whole has become highly dependent on the unions. In the fourth quarter of 2010 they accounted for 88 per cent of its income.[52] But part of the reason that the big millionaire donors were shunning the party was due to their donations to Progress. It shows how much the '"progressive rich"' demand in return for their support. Ed Miliband is simply 'not one of them', so they withdraw their funding and accumulate a nest egg of money around Progress instead. No doubt it is to be generously offered at the next election in return for a pro-business election manifesto. Contrast this attitude to the trade union leaders, who continue to give millions of pounds of their members' money to Labour and have nothing to show for it in return.

Capitalist realism is at the heart of this whole attitude of the Labour leadership. They are largely paralysed by the crisis, for it is the politics they have tailored and nurtured for at least a decade, along with the web of connections to the political and financial establishment they have accumulated, that is being strained by the crisis. To change now is politically, if not rationally, impossible as it would mean uprooting the class interests that have coloured their politics across this time.

Nonetheless, despite their relationship to sinews of capitalist power, these parties still retain their organic connection to the working class. In Britain, this connection is established through the mass of the Labour electorate and the relationship to the unions. Indeed, the alliance between Britain's moderate leaders of the big unions and the Labour leadership is a central part of the puzzle. Very few of these leaders actually shared the *ideology* of New Labour, but all of them were totally unprepared to rock the boat and have been central to the stability of the Labour Party. As grassroots activist Jerry Hicks put it, after Len Mcluskey, elected leader of the Unite union, had criticised Miliband's recent announcements on the pay freeze, "[Mcluskey] criticises aplenty and I agree with his comments, but he should have seen it coming, he has been slow to speak out, and he offers no alternative and no solution".[53]

The problem of capitalist realism, in this sense of a lack of a working class alternative to the rightward moving Labour Party, has gone hand in hand with the growing bureaucratism of the union movement, resulting in their long-term decline as effective organisations. But it is not just the Labour Party that has influenced their development. We have seen an entire transformation in the structural relationship between capital and labour. Before we consider what some of the answers might be, we'll now discuss this "new working class".

Working class, old and new

Whilst most people are quick to blame the media or the general cultural mood for influencing how others act or what they think, in fact it is often institutions that have the greatest bearing. The decline in support for the socialist left is largely the result of shifts in the working class organisations and the balance of class forces. A negative feedback loop resulted from these setbacks. The historic defeat of the British trade union rank and file in the 1980s meant that unions became more bureaucratised and less able to constitute themselves as fighting organisations. Today, socially privileged leaders of the unions advance the line of realism and moderation and help foster a wider sense that only limited forms of resistance are possible. More radical forms of resistance can appear as unrealistic in this context, while lacking anchorage and a depth of support amongst the rank and file makes it hard to win workers to radical action when the union leaders won't fight. Overall, this state of affairs compounds the isolation of the socialist left inside the labour movement.

That there has been a retreat of the left in politics and the unions is something everyone already knows. But what this actually means for us today is barely understood and little discussed, despite the transformation of the unions into fighting organisations being vital to any strategy for effectively resisting capitalism.

The economic restructuring of capital has created challenges to traditional forms of trade union organisation. The key word that has been borrowed from French by scholars and radical activists to sum up this set up changes is: *précarité*. It refers to a whole set of conditions arising from neoliberal restructuring that has increased workplace insecurity, often under the banner of creating a so-called "flexible" labour market, in which it is easier for employers to hire and fire employees as they see fit. In a recent book, *The Precariat; the New Dangerous Class,* Guy Standing analyses how neoliberalism has restructured the working class economically in a way that has deepened its alienation. Yet, he adds, it has also created new conditions that any project for radical political transformation has to take seriously.

Although Marxists of the traditional stripe have recoiled[54] at Standing's positive reference to Andre Gorz's *Farewell to the Working Class* and his appeal for a "new vocabulary... reflecting class relations in the global marketplace of the twenty-first century",[55] his neologism of choice, the *precariat,* can be seen simply as a way of capturing the precariousness of modern proletarian life and need not be incompatible with recognising the enduring central role of the "working class subject" in socialist transformation.[56] In his book, Standing highlights a series of empirically-observable changes in the relationship between labour and capital. Observing these need not undermine the idea that labour has a fundamental social power. After all, it is still the case that when labour is withdrawn on a sufficient scale then capitalists cannot profit and the system can even be paralysed. But, rather, it can be a way of understanding how capital responds to this potential. Through a multiplicity of subtle processes it creates inequality and insecurity in the working class to try and dis-incentivise mass resistance. The classical Marxist idea of a "labour aristocracy" was similarly predicated on a view that the working class was not *equal* at an economic level. It was, in fact, highly stratified and this process of differentiation has intensified across the lifespan of capitalism.

The importance of charting the increase in inequality within the working class is that this growing division is a source of stability for capital that we have to understand if we are to confront it. Jobs that we would traditionally identify as part of the industrial working class-proper have hardly been immune from the forces of *précarité.* Standing highlights how the expansion of multi-national companies has given rise to a form of "functional flexibility" that compounds job insecurity.[57] This is the ability of multi-national firms to achieve highly flexible forms of division of labour, which allows them to shift their operations from plant to plant or even country to country. Profit-maximising managers can move their operations relatively easily to boost returns, but the effect on the working class is to increase their employment uncertainty and insecurity, with the ever-present threat of relocation used to discipline the workforce. The use of outsourcing to other firms within the production process can intensify this further. Take the example of the workers at the Visteon car components plants in 2009. The work Visteon undertook was once done in-house by Ford, but by turning it into a loss-making external concern, the car maker could reduce its costs, and remove any direct responsibility it had for the workforce. This made the workers at their plants in Enfield and Belfast the first for the "chop" during the recession of 2009, as the car industry went into crisis. On this occasion, the workers fought back with factory occupations and won substantial concessions, but, unfortunately, not their jobs back.

In most industrialised countries wage-levels in real terms have stagnated since the 1970s, but this fact alone disguises the tremendous growth of inequality within the working class.

At the most general level, the decline of union power has made this possible. But there also more 'micro-level' changes in management practices that have fostered inequalities. The growth of individual contracts has been a means to deepen divisions between salaried and temporary staff, skilled and unskilled, and so on. In Japan, this process has been particularly striking for it has eroded the traditional "jobs for life" system that was an essential part of the post-war social contract. Wage levels for temporary workers in its factories are, on average, just 40 per cent those for full time staff.[58] In Britain, the long-term growth in inequality in the working class has been dramatic. As the TUC has found, "in 1977, 12 per cent of workers earned less than two-thirds of the median wage. This had risen to 21 per cent by 1998. By April 2006, more than one-fifth (23 per cent) of all UK workers – 5.3 million people – were paid less than this amount (£6.67 an hour)".[59] Changes in how capital relates to labour is one part of this picture. The other aspect is the dramatic expansion in the overall size of the workforce with the entry of women into the labour market. While of course many women have entered the professional jobs in large numbers, the more predominant tendency has been the creation of an army of low paid workers. Women represent 60 per cent of all low paid workers and, if they are in full time employment they get paid on average 17.2 per cent less than men, rising to 35.6 per cent in part time jobs.[60] It illustrates perfectly some of the contradictions of the post-68 social movements. Women won access to the workplace in vast numbers, but not on equal terms. So although the system of "male bread winners" was undermined, patriarchal assumptions about gender were expressed in new forms, particularly in super-exploitative labour market conditions. For capital, meanwhile, the entry of women in the labour market on this scale, made it possible to hold down wages per se, meaning that by the early 21st century most working class families would be dependent on two wage slips just to make ends meet.

A striking feature of the new précarité is the ease with which employers can fire workers. The growth of "zero hour" contracts – where workers don't know how much work they will be given each week, so live in constant financial uncertainty – is one of the most pernicious aspects of this system. Another is the treatment of workers as self-employed contracted individuals. The pay and conditions remain the same, but the employer loses the obligations they would have if they were hiring permanent staff, such as providing holiday pay. In the British construction industry, pyramid-like systems of sub-contracting in which one firm wins a contract, but then sub-contracts to multiple other firms to undertake the work, will often run right down to individual workers, who are then treated as self-employed subcontractors.

This system has been a key source of industrial strife in the sector over recent years. In the first Lindsey Oil Refinery strike of 2009 it also gave rise to one of the most ominous slogans seen since the recession: "British jobs, for British workers". Such demands, which illustrate how reactionary forms of ideological consciousness can arise within highly stratified workforces, are not only the preserve of the neoliberal epoch. Closed shop trade unionism in the 1960s could often be a consciously white and male affair. It reflected a division of labour that was gendered and racialised. But the fragmentation and inequalities within the working class introduced by neoliberalism has certainly created new conditions favourable to xenophobic and racist forms of divide and rule politics.

Insecurity cuts across skilled and unskilled workers, but for the most poorly paid in Britain job insecurity compounds the pain of poverty. Already in 2007, prior to the onset of the global recession, the TUC estimated that 2 million workers were in what it called "vulnerable employment", which they defined as a combination of poverty and precarious work that created a sharp "power imbalance" between workers and bosses.[61] One of the cases they reported was a mother of two, Julie, who assembled crackers as a home-maker, with an average hourly income of less than £1 with no sick pay, holiday pay, maternity pay or pension contribution, no pay slips or a written contract.[62] By 2007 there were 10 million stories similar to this. After ten years of New Labour many workers had seen very few improvements in their life. As a business model, home-working is the stuff of neoliberal dystopia - the individual is entirely atomised, stripped of rights, with seemingly little collective power, and often paid below the cost of living to boot. In this specific case, the practices were not legal and an employment tribunal eventually found in Julie's favour. This only after a toothless intervention from the Minimum Wage Enforcement Agency had made little difference.[63] In the future, however, these cases may not even be able to go to a tribunal. In November 2011 the government announced plans to reduce access to independent tribunals in favour of a "rapid resolution scheme" that would make life easier for employers. It is part of a series of measures that would deepen précarité in the labour market, including allowing dismissal without explanation and cutting the compulsory notice time for redundancies from 90 to 30 days.[64] Over three decades after Thatcher came to power, the same doublespeak argument was used to promote these measures. Making it easier to sack people will create jobs. In reality, of course, these new attacks are about deepening the exploitation and insecurity of the employed even further in a system that cannot achieve full employment.

There is, in fact, absolutely no evidence for the claim that précarité somehow tackles unemployment. On the contrary, in 1973, prior to the wave of neoliberalization of the workforce, the unemployment rate stood at less than 4 per cent, a point to which it has never since returned.[65] Although, during the globalisation boom it hovered at just above 4 per cent in the mid-2000s, real unemployment levels were disguised by the large numbers moving out of the job market altogether. During the Thatcher years, a deliberate policy of moving the unemployed onto sickness benefit would over time lead to a mushrooming in claims. In 1979, the number of sickness claimants was just 720,000[66], by 2011 this had increased to 2.6 million.[67] Behind all the big statistics are communities hit particularly hard by Thatcher's offensive. Clydebank, an old industrial town with a history of radicalism stretching back to the early 20th century, was decimated by post-industrialization in the 1980s, with unemployment spiking to 20 per cent. In the 1990s unemployment figures partially recovered, but only through a vast transfer of job seekers onto disability and sickness allowances. In 1997 unemployment had dropped to 12 per cent, but the "real unemployment rate", including the long-term sick and disabled, was now 27 per cent.[68] The enormity of this change cannot merely be put down to the conscious decisions of Tory governments to manipulate unemployment figures. It also reflects the simple fact that the politics of précarité carry costs for the physical and mental health of the exploited. The current government is determined, hypocritically given the actions of past Tory governments, to "get the sick back to work" with successive attacks on benefits. Their aim is not to actually address the social conditions that précarité has created, the physical and psychological burdens that the world of work now places on labourers, but to intensify the same policies of neoliberalization, which will further deepen alienation and poverty as hundreds of thousands, if not millions, lose their sickness benefits under the new criteria.

Life at the dole centre only adds to these pressures. "Back to work" programmes require claimants to effectively work for free, in full time posts, lest they get their benefit stopped. Following the recession of 2008 huge numbers have been compelled to this way of living. Unemployment has grown exponentially with 2.68 million, or 8.4 per cent of the workforce, now out of work.[69] A large proportion of these are aged 16 – 24 (over 1 million), making one in five young people jobless.[70] It is also the lower paid sections of the working class that are more likely to feel the pain of unemployment and move through cycles of multiple jobs. In 2009 the unemployment rate amongst senior managers and senior officials was just 3.2 per cent, while for retail workers it was 9.1 per cent, and for plant and machine operators it was 9.9 per cent.[71] The effect of all these changes has been the normalisation into the consciousness of millions that there no longer exist any "jobs for life". Instead, many have simply grown used to a precarious mode of existence, that sees them moving on and off the jobs market trying to make ends meet and get by. This whole way of life is individualised (it is up to you to "get on your bike", as Lord Tebbit infamously put it), but the circumstances and opportunities are out of our control and determined by the wider economic reality.

While it may be irrational therefore to "blame ourselves", when we suffer mental and physical collapse in the face of our apparent powerlessness, this is the exact consciousness that neoliberalism often fosters in the minds of workers. As Mark Fisher has put it:

> It is hardly surprising that people who live in such conditions - where their hours and pay can always be increased or decreased, and their terms of employment are extremely tenuous - should experience anxiety, depression and hopelessness. And it may at first seem remarkable that so many workers have been persuaded to accept such deterio-rating conditions as `natural', and to look inward – into their brain chemistry or into their personal history – for the sources of any stress... But... [in fact] this privatisation of stress has become just one more taken-for-granted dimension of a seemingly depoliticised world.[72]

Posed in these terms, we can appreciate the challenge posed by neoliberalism to the politics of radical transformation. The alienation and poverty it has fostered has changed the way that millions of workers think about their lives and one another. It has powerfully individualised even the way we think about socially-induced stress. While, as we will come onto in the next two chapters, it's important that we should not succumb to "Golden Ageism", of harking back to an illusory bygone time of working class power, the challenge nonetheless is to build new social organisations that can instil the politics of collective solidarity amongst a new generation of working class radicals. The lessons of Red Clydeside, the strip of industrial belt running from east Glasgow up the Clyde to towns like Clydebank, can only partially inform how we go about doing this. In Britain, perhaps more so than any other country, it was successive movements of organised labour that played an electric role in radicalising working class communities in the 20th century. While socialists and communists were central to these struggles, the Labour Party always stood at a safe distance from the most radical elements. Unlike other social democratic parties in Western Europe, it was never a Marxist organisation. Thus, negotiation between labour and capital, rather than confrontation, was intrinsic to Labour's whole *modus operandi*. The upshot of this conservatism was that militant trade unionism, rather than the political party of the working class, tended to play a crucial role in periods when workers radicalised.

Today, however, the unions find themselves in difficulties when it comes to the challenges posed by neoliberal restructuring. They are facing a working class which is increasingly precarious, atomized, driven away from traditional industries and towards new sectors in poorly paid, highly flexible jobs, which tend to lack a culture of trade unionism. The old 'Fordist' model of organising arose in a time of high employment and industrial strength. The in the 1950s and 1960s booming economic conditions, coupled with the Soviet threat, inclined capital to compromise, and allowed for collective bargaining and the 'closed shop' workplace, in which entry was largely controlled by powerful trade union structures. It was this entire way of organising industrial relations that Thatcher confronted in the 1980s. For we have to find organisational and political forms that recognise the new conditions brought about by post-Fordist industrialisation in these towns. The question that becomes posed, then, is what role organised labour, the "great enemy" of Thatcher in the 1980s, will play in 21st century radical politics?

The clearest indicator of the declining social power of Britain's union movement lies in the fall of trade union density (the number of workers organised). High periods of trade union membership correlate closely with high periods of strike action.

So in the 1910s, 1920s, and the 1970s, industrial strife led to workers flocking into the unions.[73] The simple reason is that waves of strike action gave the unions a sense of purpose and transformed how workers thought about their relationship with the bosses and their workmates. Indeed, 1979 did not simply represent the dawn of the neoliberal epoch, it was also a highpoint of unionisation, after huge strikes rocked British capitalism in the 1970s. A remarkable 13.2 million[74] workers were members of unions, organised into 441 unions with 109 of them in the TUC,[75] facts that made the British working class one of the best organised in the world.

Seen in these terms, we can start to understand the basis for the sense of complacency that pervaded many British unions in the 1980s. Talk to socialist activists who remember these years and they will describe the feeling of collective strength that existed, particularly in the most militant and well organised sections, like the miners, print workers and dockers. Although this reflected a justified feeling of social power, it also unfortunately fostered an illusion of invincibility. The most powerful groups of workers simply refused to believe that they could be beaten. The vast size and power of the unions by the late 1970s also illustrates the scale of the transformation that Thatcher achieved. By wiping out whole industries, bastions of organised labour, and unleashing financialization to expand new retail, services and banking sectors that were largely unorganised, the way was set for the long term decline of Britain's unions. By 2010 this meant that just 6.5 million workers[76] were organised by the unions – a decline of over 50 per cent since 1979.[77] It was only the public sector (that is the subject of major "downsizing" through austerity today), which partially withstood this offensive on the traditionally organised sectors of the working class.

Even here, though, unions became less powerful and less well-organised at the base, while "stronger" at the top, with substantial bureaucracies shaped by Thatcher's offensive.

The figures on the difference between public and private sector organisation are stark. In the public sector, unionisation rates today are 51 per cent, while in the private sector this falls to 15 per cent. This means that in 9 out of 10 workplaces in the public sector the unions will have a presence, compared to just 3 out of 10 in the private sector.[78] The decline in the scope of union power has intersected with the general pressures of individualisation fostered by neoliberalism. Together this effects how members relate to the official structures of the unions.

A general feature of individualisation within capitalist realism is what Fisher calls, "reflexive impotence"[79], or what others call "apathy". Fisher wants to avoid the moral judgement that the word apathy suggests, and try to capture the sense of powerlessness that people feel in relation to social structures, both those that exist in the workplace and in wider society. We *reflect* on our surroundings, and one another and feel our *impotence* in relation to the dominant structures. We're not apathetic, in the sense that we still *care* about society, but we just do not feel we can change it. The sense of powerlessness of ordinary workers in relation to unions exists on two levels. Firstly, poor organisation of base-level structures means that workplaces can often lack a culture of collective solidarity and day-to-day resistance to managers. This makes us more like associated individuals, rather than collective social actors with power in the workplace. Stratification inside the workplace and the culture of white collar, salaried "professionalization" further erodes the collective power of unions, by instilling instead a culture of individuals aspiring to move up the career path.

Secondly, the unions themselves are "distant" in relation to ordinary members. They send you post, they send you emails, they might even sell you insurance, but it is hard to engage with, let alone have power over, the union structure itself. This second point – the fact the unions are distant and 'above us' – actually disguises their social power.

For, where unions exist in both the public and private sector, then collective bargaining rates remain high and reflect the concentration of unions in certain sectors.[80] So, even though overall unionisation rates are low, where unions exist they tend to have collective agreements with employers. This was visible in the recent confrontation between the unions and the government over public sector pensions, which involved "collective bargaining" in its traditional form. Yet, the dispute also illustrates the problem. Ordinary members did not have any control over the negotiations or the course of the strike beyond giving their consent to it by postal ballot. Despite their collective power, then, the unions still appeared out of the reach of members. And here the key word, the key problem, is *bureaucratisation*. Overcoming it is arguably the central question facing the unions.

Unions have always had conservative bureaucracies. But the specific qualities of the union bureaucracy today emerged out of the fight against Thatcher in the 1980s. Industrial relations that were perceived to be out of control during the "Winter of Discontent" and this provided the initial spark for Thatcher's rise to power as it disillusionment with Labour was pervasive. But overtime her policies assumed a coherent logic: the deconstruction of Fordist Britain, dismantling class compromise, and restructuring capitalism through slump economics with millions thrown on the dole. The Fordist environment had afforded the unions a position of power within a state-led system of managed industrial relations, one that they were generally prepared to defend with industrial muscle as and when required.

It was this system of workplace management that capitalist ideologues started to question as the boom conditions receded into the late 1960s and early 1970s. *In Place of Strife* became a key early pre-Thatcherite text that urged the end to class compromise with legislation curtailing union rights. It influenced the first attempts to introduce anti-union laws by the Heath government in 1971, which was part of the background to the miners' strike of 1972 that brought down the Tories in 1974. As the 1970s wore on and high inflation hit the system (reaching as much as 20 per cent), successive battles were waged over wages. Across the decade rank and file militancy intersected with the revival of an anti-authoritarian Marxism following the anti-Vietnam war movement and the global uprisings of 1968. There were numerous attempts at rank and file initiatives from the cadre parties of post-War Trotskyism, like the International Socialists and the Workers Revolutionary Party. There was also a parallel revival of broad campaigns involving TUC lefts led by the Communist Party of Great Britain – still a powerful broker in the unions then.

The "Winter of Discontent" – which has achieved quite an aura in the dominant narrative of British post-war history as the moment when the populace finally lost patience with the unions – can only be understood against this longer history of 1970s radicalism. Indeed, contrary to the dominant collective memory, it was in fact working class voters who deserted the Callaghan government. They did so for the simple reason it was failing working people. For some, the reaction of this defeat was to flood into Labour so that "never again" would a government it led fail to give workers' their share. But for another section of the workers' movement the radical wing of the Labour Party posed a whole new path of development that they had no intention of pursuing. The early 1980s was, thus, a period of hope and uncertainty about what the future held. A kind of speeding up of history, with the old ways of doing things exhausted, but where multiple possible futures existed too. The conflict between Thatcher and the unions would certainly prove decisive, for it was driven forward by the powerful necessity of British capital needing to "solve" the union problem. Only occasionally did its historical nature become truly visible, and even then only amongst the most far-sighted. Yet, it was not just about the logic of capital. As time wore on and union power declined, as the initial crisis "was solved", a new ideology was born that saw marketization of every walk of life as a quasi-permanent political project: neoliberalism.

The most powerful unions were organised in the publicly owned industries. These were capitalist enterprises – they worked on the same profit/loss logic like in the market place – but state owned and managed. When Thatcher wanted to get rid of them through downsizing and privatisation, the workers' unions inevitably reacted to defend not only jobs and existing contracts, but the system of public ownership itself. It was no secret that British industry was uncompetitive. It was equally no secret that privatisation would mean dramatic restructuring at workers' expense to restore competitiveness, or simply lead to collapse in firms unable to compete with equivalent companies abroad. For the ascendant right wing ideologues of the time, it was the unions that were the source of this lack of competitiveness, it was the managers that were seen as helpless in the face of their demands, and so Thatcher's battle-cry was simply, "managers must have the right to manage". They must, in short, restore the power of capital to discipline labour. The anti-unions laws were the key part of this process. Of course there have been anti-union laws in place in Britain throughout the history of capitalism, and, since there is no constitution, workers have no "right to strike". However, the intensification of anti-union laws under Thatcher is perhaps the clearest indication of the political-social policy of monetarism, the transfer of power into the hands of the bosses and away from the workers.

The 1980 Employment Act criminalised secondary picketing – the practice of organising flying pickets to bring other workers out in solidarity with your dispute – and put restrictions on the closed shop system. The 1982 Employment Act effectively ended the closed shop system, but, most of all, it dramatically curtailed the right to strike. Secondary action (solidarity strikes) was made illegal, so too were political strikes not related to pay and conditions. If strike action was deemed illegal the union could be fined and workers sacked (partially repealing the historic immunity from compensation trade unions won in the Taft-Vale dispute of 1906). The 1984 Trade Union act made secret postal ballots compulsory, and so ended the culture of collective, shop floor strike action and deepened the process of individualisation.

The retreat sounded by the union leaders in the face of this legislation foreshadowed decades of reshaping unions around the demands of neoliberalism. It was the years 1982 to 1984 that would prove decisive in this new course. In 1982 the TUC special conference launched a campaign against the union laws, but it was reticent and cautious. General secretary Len Murray put it, "We cannot be sure that we can deliver" victory against the union laws, since Thatcher's propaganda "has even found credence among many of our members who value what their own unions do for them but are, paradoxically and illogically, at best apathetic and at worst sympathetic to the Government's purpose. We have a major job alerting trade unionists themselves to the real nature of the proposals".[81] Ultimately the trade unions were coming up against the limitations of political forms of trade union radicalism. The social power of the rank and file, its ability to deliver victories through workplace action, had once given them power over politics, but this ultimately depended on the compliance of the political and economic elite to meet their demands. The right wing split from the Labour Party, the jingo-istic fervour of the Falklands War, and the cyclical upswing of the economy, delivered a heavy Labour defeat in 1983. In the face of this, the trade union leaders had no intention of offering a political alternative on the streets.

In fact, the result of the anti-union laws was even more devas-tating in terms of how the unions saw their role in the "new order of things". Today, it is increasingly not the police and the courts that largely implement the anti-union laws, but rather the unions themselves. It is after all union leaders and officials who will be the first to try and reign in forms of direct action that break the anti-union laws when members take a dispute into their own hands. It is not, indeed, the policeman who tells the worker she cannot strike, it is instead the regional bureaucrat. This often makes union officials the first line of defence for elite and establishment interests by seeking to obstruct direct action and persecuting militants. To do so, they draw on their cultural capital, their special knowledge of the law, in order to construct an important cultural hierarchy between active, informed leaders and passive members. Understanding these ways in which unions can become "immobilisers" for working class struggle will be important to inform debates about how we win the battles ahead.

This state of affairs solidified and hardened after Thatcher came to power. At the TUC conference of 1983 the union chiefs launched a new strategy entitled "New Realism". It represented a major turning point in the history of post-war unionism and foreshadowed, indeed made possible, much of what we refer to above as *capitalist realism*. The New Realists accepted the balance of power that Thatcher established. No longer could unions be expected to bring about fundamental social change or rely on collective power, but managers would indeed "have the right to manage". The way had been prepared by people like Frank Chapple, the leader of the Electricians union, in 1982, who rejected any idea Thatcher could be defeated through extra-parliamentary struggle. Forgetting so easily the lessons militants had drawn from bringing down the Heath government in 1974, he argued that:

Those who advocate that bad laws [such as the 1982 Employment Act] should not be obeyed—in circumstances where such 'bad' laws are enacted by a democratically elected government—are putting at risk the entire conception of civilised society. That directly challenges democracy...the way to change bad laws is to change the government that has made them".[82] Len Murray echoed these words when he captured the attitude of the moderates after Labour's defeat in 1983, "we cannot talk as if the trade union movement is some sort of alternative government.[83]

This wasn't the first time union leaders had been faced with this stark choice: to resist *en masse* and attempt to mobilise millions of workers would bring into question the very stability of state power. A very similar reality was put to the unions by then Prime Minister Lloyd George in 1919, when he summoned the leaders of the Triple Alliance (the rail, transport and mining unions) into Downing Street on the eve of a massive strike.

Gentlemen, you have fashioned... a most powerful instrument. I feel bound to tell you that...we are at your mercy. The Army is disaffected and cannot be relied upon...If you carry out your strike, then you will defeat us. But...have you weighed the consequences? The strike...will precipitate a constitutional crisis of the first importance. For, if a force arises in the state which is stronger than the state... then it must be ready to take on the functions of the State itself...[84]

He added, "Gentlemen, have you considered [this] and...are you ready?" Afterwards one of the union leaders admitted: "From that moment on we were beaten and we knew we were."[85]

The "New Realism" agenda brought into focus the limitations of trade unionism as a form of politics. The nature of such institutions, rooted in workplaces and managing relations between workers' and bosses, is of not seeking to contest politics, to pursue hegemony over the wider populace and attempt to seize power in the way parties do. Across the 1980s at key moments the possibility existed for seizing back political impetus from Thatcher - the miners' strike, the defiance of Labour councils over local government cuts, the dockers and print workers' strikes. But the new policy of the trade union leaders meant they opposed with some consistency any attempt to generalise these movements into a mass strike against Thatcher's government. The result was dramatic, and delivered strategic defeats that remodelled trade unions into what Leo Panitch would later aptly call "Credit Card Unionism". They offered services such as a lawyer for tribunals, health and safety advice, and, in a sign of the times and the new globalisation era, cheap credit cards.[86] None of this stopped the decline in members, and around 5 million left between 1979 and the mid-1990s.[87]

New Realism exposed fundamental, indeed 'historical', problems with the unions. The first of these is the 'dead weight of bureaucracy'. A whole layer of officials dominates the trade unions and extract substantial material privileges from the financial contributions of ordinary members. In their great majority, they are not elected and their economic privileges tend to act as a conservative break on effective resistance. The second is the role of the union leaders as mediators between the demands of capital and the workforce. This role necessarily requires managing the antagonisms that erupt in the relationship in such a way that the social position and privileges of the bureaucracy are not undermined. This makes trade unions ideal conduits for capitalist realism. Any project of fundamental revolutionary change that sets out to do away with the exploitative relations between labour and capital necessarily threatens the position of union leaders as mediators. It was for this reason that Rosa Luxembourg once described trade union politics as the *"labour of Sisyphus"*, an unending, cumulative social struggle in the manner of the classical Greek myth.[88] This approach is naturally accordant with the politics of 'gradualism' in the post-war labour movement we have described. The problem for this outlook today is that progressive reforms are not being gradually accumulated, but capital is rather deepening *précarité* and the exploitation of labour. This should be a time when the unions come forward to do their job as defensive organisations, but so far they have only done so partially and the cause is the bureaucratic moderation that continues to fundamentally shape their practice.

Annual salary and benefits of trade union secretaries 2009-2010[89]

UNION	SALARY	BENEFITS
CWU	£87,045	£1,393
GMB	£84,000	£28,000
NUT	£111,431	£22,400
PCS	£85,421	£27,213
RMT	£84,923	£28,088
Unison	£94,953	£35,156
Unite	£97,027	£89,599
UCU	£97,592	£15,827

The salaries of union leaders far exceed the average pay of members. It means they live entirely different lifestyles from those that most workers could imagine. The figures demonstrate just how out of touch their pay is from ordinary people. The general secretary of the NUT takes home a colossal £111,431 plus benefits of £22,400. While in Unison, who organise 1.3 million largely low paid public sector workers, the equivalent figures are £94,953, plus £35,145 in benefits. Leaders of other unions are all on similar sums (see table). The median wage has oscillated, in contrast, fairly consistently at c. £25,000 a year.

The expansion of bureaucratic privileges has actually been a feature of the neoliberal age. In spite of all the anti-bureaucratic rhetoric, Thatcher's anti-union laws helped make unions far more bureaucratic than they were previously. Although trade union leaders opposed them in words, the effect of them has been to expand bureaucratic control of union structures. Partly this is due to the simple reason that these laws demanded *greater bureaucratisation* from the unions. The certification officer placed a vast number of administrative restrictions on their practices, from the registration of memberships, to accounts and the postal ballot for legal strikes. This could only expand the size and complexity of administrative systems and provide new justifications for the expansion of bureaucratic positions and the social privileges that went with them. Although the measures were presented as "democratising" the unions by making the ballots more formal, the target was never the officialdom, but the kind of grassroots, democratic organising that goes hand in hand with any militant fight back.

The TUC was not ignorant of the challenges posed by declining union density. In 1995, its then President, John Monks, launched the so-called third phase of post-war unionism, what was optimistically but tellingly dubbed "New unionism". [90] It intended to "rediscover the 'social movement' origins of labour, essentially by redefining the union as a mobilising structure which seeks to stimulate activism among its members and generate campaigns for workplace and wider social justice."[91] The pamphlet made all the right observations on the challenges posed by the new realities of globalisation. In an important sense, social movements and community-based campaigns were (and *are*) crucial to increasing union density and building renewed links with the wider working class community. But the TUC leaders were largely unprepared to draw out the more radical lessons of the 1910s, 1920s, and 1970s. Periods of mass recruitment to the unions occur when these are seen as fighting organisations, but the new way of doing politics they proposed was anathema to this. The TUC was remodelled around "public policy" discourse, and "while [it would] maintain close links with the Labour Party and broader labour movement...", it would also "actively... extend its influence across the other major political parties".[92]

Here the key word was *influence*. One of the great myths of New Realism was that capitulation to neoliberalism somehow expressed a renewal of *real influence* in the corridors of power, when it meant nothing of the sort. The new "links" proposed were only possible if they signed up to the new Thatcherite consensus.

Although the decline in trade union density stabilised slightly in the late 1990s and 2000s ("only" another million members were lost across fifteen years), the New Unionism predictably failed to reach out to the new sectors. In part, the trade union bureaucracy simply did not have the dynamism or energy to do this. However, it was also materially concerned to maintain its privileged wages and conditions, rather than funnel significant resources into organising. The answer they consequently developed to the crisis was mega-mergers. Unions that were previously "industrial" (in the sense of organising workers in a specific sector) were gobbled up into broader general unions. As a result, today there are only 58 unions in the TUC out of 154 listed on the certification officers' website. Therefore, the number of unions in the TUC has nearly halved since 1979, while the number of unions has contracted by two thirds. The big three unions (Unite, GMB, Unison) now wield a massive block vote in the TUC. Indeed, the diversity of the workforce that Unite now organises – formed out of merger between Amicus and the Transport and General Workers Union in 2007 – makes it almost a federation in its own right. This, however, has further deepened the tendency for the union bureaucracy to become more and more distant from the lives of ordinary members. With an industrial union the union bureaucracy has a much more direct relationship to the members. It is less easy for them to ignore workers' demands and easier for workers to use union structures to bring pressure to bear. All these trends are reversed with the formation of the mega-unions. That it does not address the problem of declining membership can be seen from the shocking collapse in Unite membership figures since 2007. As Martin Smith has observed, when Unite was formed it claimed to have 2 million members, but now the union's website puts it at just 1.5 million. Leaked internal documents have put the real figure at 1,182,000. In other words, if the original 2 million figure (unveiled with much fanfare at the time) is to be believed, then Unite has lost nearly a million members in five years.[93] It is a remarkable indictment of how bureaucratisation hits the organising power of the union structures.

In this way, the ideology of New Realism arose out of and extenuated the bureaucratic features of the unions by modelling them around the demands of Thatcher's laws. From the outset in 1983, it defined itself in opposition to illegal actions, which were deemed at best cavalier and at worst uncivilised. This attitude has persisted into the 21s century. In the Gate Gourmet dispute in 2005, 670 workers at the airline-catering firm were sacked by megaphone in the car park, sparking a solidarity walkout of baggage handlers at nearby Heathrow that grounded flights for three days. Fully aware that the secondary action was illegal, Tony Woodley, leader of the then Transport and General Workers Union (TGWU - a "left" union in TUC terms) played a key role in getting the baggage handlers back to work without securing the jobs of the Gate Gourmet workers. The same outlook led Derek Simpson, of Unite, to capitulate in the face of the High Court judgement that banned the British Airways strike in December 2009 on purely technical grounds (the Judge had admitted there was a legitimate mandate for action after a 90 per cent yes vote). Motivated by a concern to keep their position, to maintain their privileges, and not "rock the boat", time and again the union leaders succumb to the politics of legalism in the face of grossly unjust laws that ban *effective* trade union struggle. Indeed, the laws can often be an excuse for trade union leaders who don't want to fight. Asked on the Andrew Marr show in August 2010 whether he anticipated "Greek-style unrest"

Simpson replied, "Well I don't think that that's the nature of the British public, to be honest. I mean we don't have the volatile nature of the French or the Greeks and so on."[94] A few months later student protests shook Britain, while just over a year later 2 million trade unionists would strike, revealing their "volatile nature". But the point simply is that, for Simpson, the wish was father to the thought. His conception of the "good life" was one free of militant industrial strife, even if this meant failing to take extra-parliamentary action, which could deliver a knockout punch to government cuts. Simpson and other moderate leaders are certainly not Thatcherites, but they are very much a historical product of Thatcherism and the legacy of defeat.

We can summarise the argument presented here along four lines. Firstly, individualisation and stratification undermined the politics of collective solidarity and class struggle at the base of the unions. Secondly, the anti-union laws narrowed the legal parameters of resistance and made its most effective forms illegal. Thirdly, they also established a myriad of procedural requirements that necessitated bureaucratic expansion. Fourthly, the ideology of New Realism – effectively capitalist realism translated into the day-to-day practice of the unions – legitimised and accentuated this set of social pressures. The result is that a moderate union leadership steeped in privilege has sat atop union structures with increasingly, though certainly not entirely, passive memberships. None of this, of course, was inevitable – it arose out of the living contradictions of the class struggle in the 1980s - there were many possible outcomes if the alignment of forces had been different or if our side had better strategy.

What does this mean for the resistance to cuts today? In consonance with the politics of capitalist realism, the union leaders largely accept the logic of the cuts. They accept that cuts must be made, but they want it done under a social contract basis; to be "fairer" through the course of negotiation with union leaders. Broadly, then, the complaint is that workers are taking the *entire burden* of austerity, while the rich are feeling none of the pain and they would like this readjusted at least marginally to "share out the pain". Along these lines back in September 2010 Tony Woodley of Unite called for an Alternative Economic Strategy which would spread the cuts over 2 or 3 parliaments whilst increasing some taxes on the rich and investing in British industry.[95] Although many people will, quite understandably, react to this as a breath of fresh air amid Labour's current acceptance of the cuts, it is worth probing some of the assumptions of this argument. It calls for a return to the politics of class compromise, but on terms that are defined and set within capitalist parameters: paying back the debt to super-rich bond holders who lent money to states like Britain at their own risk. But it also comes up against the political problem: how and by what means do the trade union leaders propose to turn this into government policy? None of the mainstream parties accept this, so the union leaders would have to pro-actively fight, for example by threatening to withdraw money from Labour unless it delivers on policy, to win these changes. But the union leaders have no intention of doing so. It is not so much hot air – Woodley is no rhetorical firebrand – but words that lack any proper relationship to meaningful deeds.

If this, then, is politics without agency – i.e. without identifying how it might be achieved and the definite steps to be taken – then the wider social movement campaigning of the union leaderships has been framed by their perception of themselves as mere a-political stakeholders in a corporate world. It is again conditioned by the assumptions and legal framework established by neoliberalism that was always very clear: unions should "get out" of politics. In 2011, we saw how the union leaders were faced with a choice over how they should respond to a package of attacks. It could link them together and put a series of political demands on the government that were backed up by industrial action en masse to force concessions. But striking against the government or for a series of political policies would have been against the anti-union laws. Consequently, we have a situation in which mass, one day strikes were coordinated over public sector pensions, but only token marches of a thousand people were called by the Unite union over NHS privatisation, despite it representing a strategic attack on a service the whole working class depends on. While public sector pensions is a serious issue affecting several million people, it is not the kind of dispute which can draw in wider forces and help bridge the gap between public and private sector workers. Even when they struck on pensions, the union leaders did not raise any concrete demands on the state pension – for example, to bring the age down from 68 – or for the nationalisation of private sector pension funds to guarantee a final salary pension for all. This was "unrealistic" or rather outside the confines established by *capitalist realism* for resistance that they have accepted.

The fallout from the N30 strikes also points to a much deeper problem in the workers movement, despite the enthusiastic claims that the strike was putting "class back on the agenda" and that this marked a revival of the workers movement, the ease with which it was subsequently sold out less than a month later and the disarray that caused on the left in terms of trying to mount a credible fightback in the unions for more action indicates that N30 was simply a larger version of the common-place strikes-with-no-future. Comparisons to the General Strike of 1926 could only be made because of the numbers involved, other than that N30 represented a completely top down, controlled strike, acting more like a safety valve than a defiant struggle with the government. There was no movement from below; no significant grassroots strike committees; no direct action; and no sense that this was the start of a militant new wave of social movement resistance. The difference is often one of perspective, the left see these one day extravaganzas as the new dawn of a movement, but the people in control see it as the regrettable break down in negotiation. The left's desperate scramble for two conferences in January to "stop the sell out" attracted only a few hundred each. PCS leader Mark Serwotka spoke at both but even at his most adventurous he talked about a smaller coalition-of-the-willing to take action later in March. But even that proved too much for the PCS executive, who pulled out of any co-ordinated strikes at the end of the month on the promise of another strike at a later date. The dispute ended not with a bang but with a whimper. The defeat of the pensions struggle is another nail in the coffin of the trade union movement in its current, highly conservative form. Surely, it is time to reject the logic behind these one-day extravaganzas; these strikes with no future, strikes of protest foreshadowing defeat and rotten compromise.

This conservatism of the union leaders, and the social privileges that underline it, is the central problem facing the unions. For the union leaders have largely accepted that an ever-greater encroachment of capital into our lives is inevitable, so they are engaged simply in a war of attrition with it and have no desire to ultimately stop and reverse it, let alone takes steps to a fundamentally different system. The only conclusion that we can draw is that the unions have to be transformed if they are to be fit for purpose. The role of the union leaders in the recent pensions dispute shows us the simple problem that they are prone to sell out rather than fight. Even when they do fight it is by launching "a strike with no future", a one-day spectacular that does not force any serious concessions from the government.

In Britain, the unions are strongest in the public sector, which grew quite considerably under New Labour. They are weaker in the private sector - which points to the real problem of labour organisation today. It is private sector workers that produce value and therefore wealth. When they strike they hit the capitalists where it most hurts, in their pockets/profits. Public sector workers are part of the service sector, but not directly engaged in profit creation of the distribution of commodities on the market. A days strike by public sector workers does not frustrate profit creation, except as a collateral factor, for instance when private sector workers with children have to take the day off work when schools are shut.

As the spectre of unemployment grows more workers feel afraid to stand up for their rights and interests. The unions, usually tied to the social democratic parties, offer piecemeal resistance to the austerity attacks, and try to overcome declining numbers through more and more mergers into mega unions – dominated by mega bureaucracies. Whilst the bosses attack in a co-ordinated and ruthless fashion, the working class leaders have largely proven themselves to be loyal lieutenants of capital – the see their jobs as managing the transition, to negotiate and to ameliorate the worst affects. But they accept that the cuts must happen – just more slowly and more gently. Those union leaders who want to fight are afraid to pull out all the stops, whereas the centre and right union leaders are desperate not to struggle – they urge compromise and negotiation. The lack of an alternative can be seen in the weasel words of the leaders of the labour movement – they are business realists, they often just want everyone to do their bit whether it is to pay more taxes or work longer hours: "in times of crisis we have to keep the [or rather "their"] economy going".

The rough strategic outline for a radical re-organisation of the workers movement could look something like this. Transforming the unions means beginning the campaign to build grassroots co-ordinations of the members that moves towards a position of dual power between an active and mobilised grassroots membership and the bureaucrats. This process requires a united front with the leaders to take action, but constant and systematic moves to build co-ordinations and networks that can take action when the leaders sell out. This should not be done under some party front umbrella, run by the industrial department of one of the sects, it needs to be democratic and above all *authentic,* a real expression of working class self-activism. Any movement that seeks a serious struggle against the cuts would inevitably confront both the power of the government, the union machinery and the courts. But that means it is doing its job, since these are precisely the three foes whose authority has to be challenged if we are to win.

Finally, beyond the immediate struggle of the public sector workers, we have to think into the medium and long term about where the working class is growing and how to build effective unions there. The unions find the new precarious sectors are hard to organise. In many workplaces, especially in low skilled sectors where the workers are mainly young, unions are almost unheard of. Many workers prefer to move jobs rather than stay and fight to improve conditions, reflecting the kind of attitude workers had in the late 19th century compared to the post war industrial working class.

If the unions fail to save the public sector then a proverbial guerrilla war will emerge as privatisation will inevitable see union recognition deals ripped up, forcing workers to switch tactics and focus energies on organising under the whip of capital instead of simply managerial bureaucracy, as is the case in the current public sector arrangement.

The balance to be struck is recognising and relating to the changing nature of working life, the new conditions and challenges posed by the current moment, without denying the enormous social power that unions still have. They are, in some respect, the most powerful non-state actors in Britain, with a membership essential to the production, circulation and distribution of goods and services. But their concentration in the public sector limits the extent to which they can really hit the profit system. Transforming the unions must mean turning them outwards to the new layers of more precarious and super-exploited working class that neoliberalism has created. But it also means doing this in parallel to building grassroots organi-sation that challenges the control of the bureaucratic elites at the top. It's this combination of a political perspective, social movement and community organisation and grassroots, "rank and file" democracy and movements that can deliver real change.

2011: Protest and power

When *Time* magazine made "The Protester" their person of 2011 they wrote:

> All over the world, the protesters of 2011 share a belief that their countries' political systems and economies have grown dysfunctional and corrupt — sham democracies rigged to favour the rich and powerful and prevent significant change. They are fervent small-*d* democrats. Two decades after the final failure and abandonment of communism, they believe they're experiencing the failure of hell-bent mega scaled crony hypercapitalism and pine for some third way, a new social contract. [96]

It is difficult to fault this as an understanding of 2011. The movements of the Arab Spring, the *indignados* of Spain and Greece, and Occupy Wall Street, all shared a common conviction that democracy remained out of the grasp of the people. While in the Middle East and North African uprisings, the rulers confronted were old-fashioned clientelist despots and the protesters thus aspired to a system of universal suffrage, the demand for social and economic justice still acted as a common thread uniting struggles across these continents. In the West, protestors challenged ruling elites that had grown accustomed to political systems in which the neoliberal centre had expanded to such a degree that evenly marginally different economic programmes had been pushed out to the fringe. As a result, it was to the streets that these perspectives had to go and the result was popular movements that acted as a focal point for discontent with a system colonised by the "bankocracy" of Wall Street.

Given the origins of these movements as responses to economic injustice, the emergence of them in 2011 cannot be understood outside of the rhythms of the global capitalist crisis and the spiralling anger at inequality in many states of the world; particularly, in Europe, US, and Middle East. But they share a common ethos that *Time* magazine summed up as a pining for a third way, "a new social contract". It is the nature of that social contract which is now being negotiated but a great deal ambiguity exists over what its exact form should take and the diverse ways in which this idea is even conceived from one country to another. The problem confronting elites and subaltern movements is: can capitalism afford the most minimal of their demands? Can the existing neoliberal model integrate the discontented?

If we look simply at the wealth accumulated by the rich in the last decades we might well answer 'yes' as the sums are quite astronomical. Indeed, while we might quibble with the specific slogan of the 1 per cent – not least because the top five or ten per cent of US society live in immense luxury too – it nonetheless was particularly appropriate rallying call in the American context, because the super-rich have grown astronomically wealthy at the expense of the rest. Back in 2007 for example, the top 1 per cent had more financial wealth (your net wealth less the value of your home) than the bottom *95 per cent.*[97] By focusing attention on the super-rich it provided a startling opportunity to open a debate about class interests in American politics. Of course, Occupy as a conception was always necessarily limited; its tactic of choice – the city centre camp – was unsustainable in the long-term. All such movements that involve frequent and intense forms of direct action, from occupations to other forms of civil disobedience, will generate a burst of activity fuelled by the adrenalin of participants, which then has to give way to a period of contemplation and recovery.

While Occupy was at times derided (by left and right wing commentators alike) for not having a worked out set of policies, its generality and amorphousness actually amplified its social power. The simple point that politics had become an instrument of the material interests of the top 1% represented a profound challenge to three decades of economic policy in the West. Many of the statistics the occupiers pointed to had long been available, but with a rising tide of home dispossessions and unemployment they became fixed in the popular imagination of millions of US workers. How could it be that the world's richest and most affluent country could allow a situation to persist in which 400 individuals – each of them dollar billionaires – could control more wealth than 60 per cent of American workers?[98] The story of American neoliberalism is a story of rising inequality; and as we have already recounted the post-2008 policy measures are designed to protect the financial structures that maintain this divide. So even though Occupy did not start out with a pre-determined sense of what the answers were, if it had done so then it is unlikely to have succeeded in capturing popular consciousness in the way that it did. It is a worked example of how in the opening stages of a process sometimes just to ask a question that no one has been asking can open up new avenues for a more radical, far-reaching political change. A more-worked out set of political demands would not have been able to have anything like the same effect. It was the simplicity of the Occupy message that struck a chord. These are precisely the kinds of movements that the organised left should look to develop in order to gain a wider hearing for a more worked out political strategy that can transcend capitalism.

Here, however, comes the rub. Had an organised section of the left – say, hypothetically, the American International Socialist Organisation – called for the formation of a 20,000-strong tent city in Wall St, then it would have in likelihood been met with derision. No serious left wing organisation would have been so foolish as to do this, but it illustrates the problem with how socialist ideas still don't form part of a natural *Zeitgeist*. This isn't only true of the United States, where radical socialist ideas never had the "organicity" in the working class that they once enjoyed in Europe, but it is a general problem that socialists confront. The challenge is how to introduce this politics into these mobilisations so that it does not appear as a fringe movement, but act as an organically emergent phenomenon from 'within'. The tension that needs to be recognised is the need to build social movements that strike a chord – around therefore necessarily limited demands or even just simple ideas – but also seeking to develop from within them, as a natural part of them, a socialist consciousness.

If we look at the origins of OccupyWallSt it is useful to see how activists succeeded in capturing the 'spirit of the times' with a timely appeal to act. One influence on Occupy was simple old fashioned international solidarity; the semi-globalisation of the Tahir Square encampment to the US, Spain and Greece. This inspiration was quite explicit for those in North America that made the call back in July 2011. It originally came from *Adbusters,* a Vancouver-based radical magazine originally founded amidst the very earliest anticapitalist mobilisations of the early 1990s that would later spiral into the Seattle protests. For some of us, they are a blast from the past; recalling an age when Naomi Klein's *No Logo* challenged the mushrooming reach of corporate identities in the Clinton era. But in 2011 these groups achieved a breadth of appeal in the United States that went far beyond Seattle '99.

In an interview with *Salon* magazine Kalle Lasn, *Adbusters* editor, described how they were influenced by the Egyptian Revolution but also saw how with rising joblessness and poverty had not led to "the people who gave us this mess", "the financial fraudsters on Wall Street" being "brought to justice" and so "felt this was the right moment to instigate something."[99] In a sense, this was traditional popular 'agitation' familiar to Marxists, but it is interesting that Lasn went on to ground *Adbusters'* approach in 1968 French Situationist philosophy:

We are not just inspired by what happened in the Arab Spring recently, we are students of the Situationist movement. Those are the people who gave birth to what many people think was the first global revolution back in 1968 when some uprisings in Paris suddenly inspired uprisings all over the world. All of a sudden universities and cities were exploding. This was done by a small group of people, the Situationists, who were like the philosophical backbone of the movement. One of the key guys was Guy Debord, who wrote 'The Society of the Spectacle.' The idea is that if you have a very powerful meme — a very powerful idea — and the moment is ripe, then that is enough to ignite a revolution.[100]

For those who know their 19th and 20th century radical history then it is easy to recoil in horror at some of these formulations. 1968 *was not* the first global inferno of its kind. Similar globally dispersed but interconnected, indeed seemingly almost "synchronised", movements emerged in 1848, between 1917 and 1920, and even at the close of the Second World War. And as good sociologists, Marxists will emphasise the role of circumstances, conditions, social and economic processes, transformation in culture, ideology and values, and not just the role played by the single idea. But this should not blind us to the element of truth that Kalle Lasn and *Adbusters* emphasise; that the right idea, put across in the right way, in the right circumstances, with the right alliances, can have this trigger effect, where it spirals out of control and suddenly grips mass consciousness. Seen in this way, *Adbusters* alerts us to the importance of using modern language, of being bold but popular, of taking care to find ways of putting across ideas that really resonates.

At times over the last decade the organised socialist left in a number of countries has been able to play a similar role. Socialists in the National Campaign Against Fees and Cuts

(NCAFC) in Britain during the student movement put out a call for mass walkouts and protests that similarly struck a chord. In the anti-war movement in 2002 and 2003 the organised left were also at the heart of it. These simple appeals for action were able to strike a chord with mass consciousness. They were presented to wide layers without demanding any predefined commitment to an ideology but simply appealed to a shared notion of injustice. In a sense, who put out the call – whether it is *Adbusters* or socialists embedded within a campaign – is neither here nor there, because we are talking about situations that were crying out for such a move. *Adbusters* just had the foresight to make the right call at the right time.

Talk to activists involved in Occupy in the United States and they will tell you that many of its "cadres", i.e. those really at the heart of the protests, often traced the origins of their political activism back to the anticapitalist mobilisations around Seattle. These networks of activists had remained in existence, producing magazines, launching episodic direct action campaigns, and so on, since the huge protests over a decade ago. And there is an important similarity between Occupy and the anticapitalist movements of those years, insofar as they share this "meme" appeal; the idea is at once simple, popular and appealing, but it also introduces a complex argument about the nature of capitalism. Some activists in these movements see them as having a "prefigurative" nature, of creating spaces that simulate future utopias, something which accords with the Situationist ethos of *Adbusters.* But they also bring together a broad spectrum of ideological outlooks, from varieties of anarchism and libertarianism, to reformist currents. Organised forms of socialist politics, though, still remain a fringe element within these protests, even if there is a revival of interest in some of the ideas, most activists are not attracted to the kind of party structure that the left adopts.

This reflects challenges of the post-1989 epoch, but socialists can also be the own worst enemy when it comes to trying to introduce their ideas in an "organic" way within these movements. As the American writer and socialist Pham Binh observed, the organised American left tended to see their role in Occupy in propagandistic terms; of introducing a new layer of activists to Marxist doctrine and so they focused their energies on running the political programme of the "occupy university" or its equivalents, of organising fringe meetings on the role of the police within the capitalist state, and so on.[101] While this is all perfectly rational at one level, the form of the intervention was of socialists presenting their ideas to a non-socialist movement, rather than actually thinking about how the same politics could be put across in a way that it suddenly appeared a natural ideology for any one that is serious about moving beyond capitalism. Indeed, we could do with learning from *Adbusters*; of thinking how we can actually distil the wider political "programme" into similarly effective *memes* i.e. powerful ideas – that strike a chord with the consciousness of the movement. The question of how we go from limited "agitation", i.e. campaigning around immediate issues, to popularising an ideology is the central problem here. For, while socialists are good at striking a "united front" around single issues – stop the cuts, no fees, end the war, and so on – they are less good at formulating simple ideas that are able to both capture popular opinion and also imply a far reaching critique of the capitalist system.

The differences between the Arab Spring and the Occupy movement are ultimately tremendous; in the demands, the circumstances, and the challenges confronted. But the same problem still presents itself to the radical left; of how to move from social movement agitation to making radical left wing and anticapitalist politics a credible force. In both cases, it is easy to explode the myth of spontaneity – the idea that these protests emerged seemingly out of nowhere as a rupture within the existing order. For both the Arab Spring and Occupy can be traced to inter-connecting sets of causes and circumstances across the last decade. In Occupy activist movements from the 1990s – armed with a simple meme informed by a Situationist philosophy – suddenly found an echo for their ideas on a far larger scale due to the new circumstances of the post-Lehman Brothers world. In the Arab Spring a longer process of accumulating discontent and mobilisation intersected with the crisis that engulfed the global economy after 2008. Here too the movements which emerged out of the instability were at once local and global, for even in their earliest origins they were imbued with a powerful sense of international solidarity. Indeed, the Egyptian socialist, Hossam el-Hamalawy, identifies the solidarity movement with the Palestinian Intifada in 2000 as a critical turning point for the Mubarak regime as the toleration of it by the authorities ended the period of bitter state crackdown and street fighting with Islamists in the 1990s.[102] Between 2006 and 2008 many writers had started to identify the new democracy movements running in parallel to a wave of strikes and with them the development a nucleus of independent unions organising separately from the state unions of the regime.

One book that has a particular claim to have predicted the Egyptian Revolution back in 2009 is Rabab El-Mahdi and Philip Marfleet's *Egypt: the Moment of Change,* a collection of essays that traced how growing social inequalities arising from neoliberal modernisation, had interconnected with rising workers' struggles and new democracy movements, laying the potential for a perfect storm scenario that would bring enormous pressure to bear on the regime.[103] But, although these processes foreshadowed 2011, we still find a similar trigger effect "meme" moment during the Arab Spring. The inspiration of the Tunisian Revolution encouraged democracy activists onto the streets where they combined oft-recounted mobilisations through Twitter and Facebook with old-fashioned agitation for social and economic demands in the slums of Cairo and Alexandria. Here the "meme effect" was quite extraordinary with literally millions coming out on the streets in February 2010. Tunisia had shown what was possible and thus activists were able to capitalise upon the causal efficacy of hope, as the *belief* that Mubarak could be dislodged brought people onto the streets. It was a classical revolutionary inferno similar in scale to the vast mobilisations of workers and students in Tiananmen Square in 1989. The "moment of change" came as a crescendo forcing an initially conservative military apparatus to move against the Mubarak regime.

Unlike, each in their own way, Libya, due to western intervention, and Syria, due to the uneven distribution of political radicalism within the polity that has helped to sustain the Assad regime, Egypt, has followed closely the classical patterns of revolution: of mass mobilisation, creating the uncertain moment where force could be used to suppress the people, followed on this occasion by the actual overthrow of the despot, feeding into an interregnum phase in which conservative forces seek to obstruct the aspirations of the people through democratic or violent means, or some combination of the two. In Egypt, a principal actor in this regard, which stood carefully with "one foot in and one foot out" of the original revolution, is the Muslim Brotherhood that won a landslide victory in parliamentary elections, largely on the promises of economic and social reform. Its role illustrates the problems of Situationism as a strategy, because it underlines the episodic nature of the meme effect. The moment of mass mobilisation cannot endure forever at which point the masses will fall back on their existing institutions. The political lesson lies in what Antonio Gramsci called "the war of position", of trying to build, over the long-term, durable political organisations that have deep roots in society, so that when the moment of crisis and mass mobilisation emerges, they are in a position to make what once appeared to be the politically impossible become the politically inevitable. In short, organisations with social weight are in a position to politically capitalise after the meme-moment subsides.

Notwithstanding the challenges the post-1989 world poses to socialist politics, here again the historical disunity of the left hampers its attempts to build parties with real social power. There is no point bemoaning lost time, let alone harking back to an illusory golden age of socialist politics prior to the collapse of the Soviet Union. The death of Stalinism as a state-ideology is something that should be warmly welcomed and all periods of modernity have seen opportunities and challenges juxtaposed to one another. But we do need to start to re-organise radical left wing politics so that we can begin to put down deeper roots in society. The fact we have to do this in a period of accelerated social change – in which crisis and political disequilibrium has become a "normalised" part of life – rather than a period of greater stability that might be more conducive to "preparation", is the simple reality of where left wing politics is. At least in such periods of crisis, the potential for a wide-reaching transformation in working class consciousness is much greater than in normal times.

The process of establishing forms of organisation that can renew the socialist project has to recognise, on the one hand, that the left has an obligation to move beyond its existing state of disunity and gets its "own house in order", but also, simultaneously, should look beyond the left to new layers of activists many of whom will not consider themselves socialist. One of the questions that the new movements of 2011 posed sharply is the relationship between traditional left-wing ideology and the "new left" libertarianism. The latter should not be confused with anarchism, which is a distinctive body of ideology in its own right, whereas the new libertarianism is much more of a *Zeitgeist* that reflects disillusionment with traditional forms of revolutionary socialist politics and organisation. The new libertarians' concern for individual rights, and democratic and participatory forms of organisation, reflect their desire to avoid radicals inadvertently stumbling into the authoritarianism that blighted 20th century left wing politics. The preference of the new left for "horizontal" methods of organising, on reclaiming spaces with occupations, has often made them the most dynamic, freshest, and youngest elements of the renewed anticapitalist movements. Many of their criticisms of the "old left", such as the frustrations with its organisational divisions into competing sects, hold true. And the best of this layer are often looking for practical answers to the problems they confront, are attracted to Marxism when it can show that it is a guide to such action, and are invariably put off it when the left simply appear to be deducing their political conclusions from an abstract set of predefined, abstract and dogmatic assertions

The positive side of the libertarian movement is easy to see. It has a DIY attitude, is unencumbered by the conservative and highly bureaucratic hierarchies of the workers' movement, and utilises direct action. But it is not just these practices that make the new left appear attractive. They are also able to present their ideas as un-impinged by the old debates between the Trotskyists and the Stalinists, and so un-tarred with the brush of defeat that the old hierarchies suffered in the 20th century. The working class movement too is considered one amongst many oppressed communities – such as women, Black or LGBTQ – and, insofar as this reflects the defeat of *labour* politics, it chimes with the post-1989 world.

Their non-conformity with traditional left wing ideology also chimes with the post ideological age, for it is a general trend in the West that new layers of young people who see the need to fight capitalism are particularly conscious of past failures, are often agnostic to the traditional hierarchies, particularly political parties, and see de-centralised social movements as the answer. This isn't classical anarchism, whose political organisations can often be more marginalised than the socialist left, but is a general sensibility amongst the young people joining today's demonstrations. Indeed the lack of substantial growth of organised anarchism is illustrative of the fact that these new layers of activists are not joining political organisations *per se*. Given that this constituency is crucial to any organised left wing project their concerns – their reasons for *not "signing up"* – quite simply have to be addressed.

To do this, we will need to move away from the tendency to see the "new" and "old" left as irreconcilable opposites. The relationship between the "Trotskyist paper sellers" and the "libertarian movement activists" is a complex one. Both sides of this dichotomy draw together elements that will need to be incorporated into a revivified anticapitalist politics. The traditional left can be routinist, conservative and dogmatic, because its structures of choice, the top-down political party-model, lacks flexibility and sees its job as sustaining a certain set of ideas and model of doing politics. The organisational model is directly related to the lack of ideological plurality in how their politics tend to be conceived; usually in terms of a single "right" or "wrong" answer – with a lack of tolerance, in the literal sense of "slack", which is needed to open up to wider perspectives. But these negatives also give it the ideological stability that networks tend to lack; the latter famously "come and go" with high and low points of social struggle, whereas the Leninist grouping carries on meeting and organising even in the troths of mobilisation. Party forms of organisation also act as "the memory of the class" in the sense that they keep alive a vision of a fundamental alternative to capitalism, an egalitarian socialist order, and educate their memberships in the lessons their particular ideological trend has derived from past experiences of social struggle. These working class traditions lead the left to prioritise the long and often unrewarding task of establishing footholds within the labour movement – a key part of the "war of position" conception that requires long-term work to put down real social roots – and horizontalists, in contrast, tend not to undertake this activity. This follows naturally from the theoretical assumptions that favour the meme-moment over longer-term strategy, because once the social world is conceived in largely spontaneous terms, and the single, powerful idea seen as having dramatic causal power, then putting down social roots becomes much less relevant.

The spectacular success of Occupy is only one amongst many actions that the new left has pulled off over the years. Reclaim the Streets in the 1990s initiated a number of anticapitalist protests, including the J18 shut down of the City of London, and across the 2000s the autonomist and libertarian left organised a series of alternative camps and protests outside the G8. In Britain, we saw the rise of Climate Camp, which was like Occupy in the sense it was able to strike a chord with much wider layers of working class people. No socialist is likely to deny that there is a dynamism and flair to these movements, but it is perhaps more controversial to recognise that this might be directly related to the participatory forms of organisation that they favour. The stage-managed left wing meeting creates a culture and, indeed an aesthetic – the way that it looks and feels – that is highly conservative. In contrast, the participatory democracy of the new social movements has a genuine freshness and appeal. Recognising this is so important to renewing socialist ideas.

But for all its positive qualities we should not romanticise the "new left" nor see only negatives in the methodology of traditional socialists. Recognising the role played by forms of modified consensus in building open, fraternal and pluralistic political organisations is essential to building trust and new forms of unity amongst socialists. Yet there is also an age old tendency amongst some new left activists to see consensus as an absolute principle – an ironic thing in itself as it can often be the issue "on which no consensus is allowed". The long "General Assembly" meetings of Occupy can ultimately be exclusive, because those that last the longest and stick it out to the end will get their way. Leave because you have to go to work, or have some other commitment, and you lose your say. Needless to say that this has obvious "class consequences" for this form of organisation to draw in working class people.

On the million-dollar question – "what has the new left achieved strategically" from Seattle to Occupy – the new left can answer no more confidently than the socialist left. It is also debateable whether the new left has what we might call a "strategic project", defined organisations, and a political agenda. The lack of these can be a positive in the early phases of a radicalisation, but they can also become negatives as politically challenges intensify. In some countries, the libertarian left is also still plagued by a "propaganda of the deed" type ethos that substitutes individual acts, such as property damage, for the collective organisation and power of working people.[104] On 26 March TUC day of action in Britain, we saw how foolish black bloc actions stole the headlines and were met with universal condemnation from the low paid public sector workers marching in their hundreds of thousands. There could be few better examples of how *not* to relate radical politics to the wider working class; indeed, it is a method that is designed for *irrelevance in perpetuity.*

The positive side of the current conjuncture is that it exposes the limitations in the political practices and philosophy of the organised left and the libertarian activist milieu simultaneously. A growing number of activists, who might be labelled "libertarians" and "Trots" depending on what side of this divide you are on, are starting to question the limitations of their preferred forms of organisation. If activists from the libertarian left are starting to see that that social power of the organised working class action is crucial to the resistance to austerity, then new organisational forms can also start to overcome other differences. For the "old left" far less dogmatism in their organisational and ideological assumptions coupled with genuine attempts to build organic unity amongst socialists would go a long way to reach a situation where we no longer treated "old" and "new" as dichotomies.

This does not mean that it must eclectically muddle irreconcilable positions, but by adopting an open-minded disposition, one that recognises that practice is the main criteria for truth,[105] and finding points of agreement with the best "libertarian" activists we can begin the process of renewal. If we identify key points of agreement we can also lay down parameters for a new radical project. A crucial starting point will be to bring together those that recognise that political organisation is needed and that we have to address the question of power even if we disagree on whether a political party of the working class is needed.

After all, another common thread across the protests movements of 2011 is that they all confronted "the power question". Positive and negative expressions of this abound. In the revolutionary inferno of Egypt, Mubarak was dislodged by the people but power had not passed into their hands for the military high command assumed the authority that Mubarak had once claimed to have over them. In the Occupy encampments of the West the existence of power was felt with a much explicit negativity: as the alienation of subaltern layers from the citadels of neoliberal state power. For the *Indigandos* of Spain this fed a mistaken propensity for "anti-politics", where political demands were seen as aspiring to achieve a form of power that would merely reproduce subordination. It is perhaps the worst of all possible conclusions to draw. Should we promote the myth that we can create a prefigurative space within capital that has a liberating function somehow outside the power relations of the system, we will actually reinforce the sense of powerlessness that capital imposes on us. How, after all, can we fight for the jobs of single Spanish youth – some 50 per cent of whom are unemployed – if we do not demand investment over austerity? If we bring together in common organisations layers of activists who are not "anti-politics", but see the need for it, then we can start to formulate a credible strategy for radical social change.

A challenge we will face is how to respond to the demands for a "new social contract". We need to think about transitional forms of political struggle that open up avenues for working class empowerment and force crises of capital. But we also need to be aware of the enduring allure and power of capital to pacify social protest and incorporate our demands into "social contracts" however illusory. Today, however, this may be less easy to achieve than it once was. A social contract either on the model of the Keynesian post-war boom of the 1950s and 60s or on model of the neoliberalised "commodity individualism" of the 1980s, both confront enormous structural obstacles. The conditions that made the social compromise unattractive for capital emerged in the crisis of the 1970s. Labour and capital had realised fruits from growth throughout the post-war boom but as crisis returned to the system, the restructuring of labour relations and industry on pro-market lines broke the social compromise and ultimately put the unions into a long cycle of retreat. But a new "social contract" still emerged, which was based upon the ideology of market individualism and underscored by mushrooming debt levels. It was able to make up for stagnating working class incomes and further compounded the long retreat of organised labour. Whether debt will be able to play this role in the future looks highly unlikely at the current moment. Certainly, figures will come forward, in the way that France's Francois Hollande has done, promising a new social contract based upon some form of redistribution, but they will confront extraordinary structural obstacles in the capitalist economy: can capital "afford it"? The answer is likely to be transmitted through the subterranean conduit of the fluctuating financial markets in order to set narrow parameters for policy on western governments.

In May 2012, activists from Occupy launched the *Global Mayday Manifesto* – an exciting initiative that was a part of

2011: Protest and power

process to define what the movement stood for. It was written with eloquence and simplicity. The style and tone was a model for any radical manifesto, creating a sense that the movement was going forward, appealing directly to the modernist ideal of progress – "the values of liberty, equality, and fraternity, the old dream of our ancestors when they rose against oppression" – and capturing the democratic ethos, the desire to combine individual and collective rights, that had imbued Occupy. A list of democratic and social demands followed. In its totality these demands would not unseat capitalism, but each and every one of them could be utilised as the basis for mass mobilisations out of which a more socialistic, radical consciousness might be fostered.

The radical democratic ethos of Occupy actually recalls some of the best traditions of the classical social democratic movement. For while it is true that if the *MayDay Manifesto* was won *in toto* this may not *necessarily* go alongside a transcendence of capitalism, its demands are very far from complimentary to the capitalist order. It is similar, in this regard, to the old "minimum" programme of the Marxist social democracy in the late 19th and early 20th centuries. The *Erfurt Programme* of the German social democracy put forward a set of radical democratic demands many of which have still not been won; such as the call for two year legislative parliaments, proportional representation in elections, and annual referenda on levels of taxation. The term "minimum" was a little misleading, because this platform represented the *maximum possible* democratic and social rights that could in principle be realised within a capitalist system. The fact that many of these rights have not yet been secured, or won only to then be lost, illustrates how democracy is a far from "natural" bedfellow of the capitalist system of production. This is why the fight for democratic demands and social rights – particularly when this is taken into the workplace to directly challenge capitalist power – opens up antagonisms with capitalist ruling elites.

The *Erfurt Programme* provides important guidance for how Marxists should approach the *MayDay Manifesto*. It once said that socialists do "not fight for new class privileges and class rights, but for the abolition of class rule and of classes themselves, for equal rights and equal obligations for all, without distinction of sex or birth. Starting from these views, it fights not only the exploitation and oppression of wage earners in society today, but every manner of exploitation and oppression, whether directed against a class, party, sex, or race."

In this spirit, Occupiers have put forward a new, popular minimum programme pushing in the direction of a different kind of society. But it does this in the context of a universal expansion of liberal democracy since 1989. This is why each and every one of its calls for local and global democratisation of human life involves a profound critique of the status quo order: "'Democratic' political systems, where they exist, have been emptied of meaning, put to the service of those few interested in increasing the power of corporations and financial institutions, regardless of the fate of the planet and its inhabitants." Using situations wracked with social crisis, such as we have seen in Greece over the last five years, as a testing ground, we need to push these movements in the direction of radical forms of workplace democracy, co-ordinating new forms of collective, democratic and participatory working class organisation, that challenges the power of the capitalist state, and can ultimately provide the basis for a new type of society. This will of course, mean extending the Occupy manifesto dramatically, but it explicitly defines itself as a "process of global dialogue", a "work-in-progress", and through building thoroughly democratic and popular mass movements with the Occupiers a new generation might come to socialist conclusions.

Occupy has challenged the specific form of liberal "representative" – i.e. above the people and relatively unaccountable to the people – model of democracy and has opened up an avenue for more far-reaching, socialist visions. The demands of the *MayDay Manifesto* in particular extend this to the sphere of private property – normally outside any democratic control. Most important, perhaps, was its calls to extend democratic rights down to the workplace level, in the form of movements that utilised the tactics of Occupy to challenge the hegemony of the capitalist on their own terrain. In so doing, it unconsciously recalled earlier attempts by Marxists to formulate "transitional demands" that empowered the working class in relation to capital, could be momentarily won through resistance, but were ultimately unstable unless an anticapitalist transformation could be realised.

Occupy is not therefore underpinned by "liberal" discourse. It is much more complex than that; for its activists are attempting to formulate a democratic and anticapitalist politics that does not lapse into the authoritarianism of the last century. Marxists should to be trying to give these formulations a class struggle and socialistic logic organically so that they emerge as a new kind of "common sense" for the movement. Indeed, Occupy serves as a continual reminder of how important democracy and participation is to the renewal of a healthy socialist project; not only to ensure its ultimate success, but also, in the much shorter-term, for it to have any hope of gaining a wider hearing amongst a new generation of left activists.

The obvious question this poses is what relation does the fight for democracy have to revolutionary social change today? If this question is treated as a merely formal one, then they are likely to be seen as two different kinds of revolutions. Democratic movements are normally regarded as seeking political revolution; a change in the structures of the ruling elites and the opening up of a greater popular democracy. A socialist revolution is a *social* revolution, one that puts a new class in power. We could see the political revolutions of today as the modern equivalent of the storming of the Bastille in 1789 – the promise of the bourgeois epoch made manifest again – but their contradiction lies in the fact that they challenge the *narrowly conceived* and *insufficient* democratisation that capitalism has realised. Indeed, in 1789 the French revolution was a social revolution in the proper sense of the term. But its promise of equality and far-reaching democratisation was undermined by the new market-based exploitations that it unleashed. This is not to say that the political terrain exists in a merely axiomatic relationship to class interests; but the class structure of capitalist society will often condition the terrain of what is "acceptable". It does so through subterranean mechanisms, such as whether markets have "confidence" in governments to create political and social conditions favourable to business, which fuse direct economic power – such as driving the cost of borrowing – with naturalising bourgeois ideology.

Many generations later we can see how liberal democracy has fostered a distinction between the political elites and the disempowered mass of voters who can exercise a say over government only once every so many years. Our world is consequently an increasingly post-democratic one, not because there are no elections but because the elections mean less and less. And this is due to the decline of class forces that use to contest capitalism politically in one way or another; either be promoting a progressive social reform agenda that narrowed the space for capitalists profiteering by expanding the state, or more revolutionary challenges to the hegemony of the global marketplace. This is why one way of thinking about neoliberalism is as a dramatic intensification of the "natural" tendencies of capitalism as political forces that contested it have subsided. The result is a narrowing of the *acceptable* terrain of mainstream politics around neoliberal assumptions; such that the *spectacle* of politics assumes a primacy over and above its ideological *content*.

The proof of this is not hard to find. The promise of "change" and "hope" offered up by the Obama election campaign now looks unbelievably facile and meaningless. There has been little substantial social change in American since his presidency. But in countries that have suffered acute levels of social hardship, such as Greece, the disjuncture between the disempowered mass of voters and the political elite that is entirely out of touch is all the more obvious. Greek voters over several elections have challenged and even thrown out pro-austerity, corrupt govern- ments, but they got in return ever-greater austerity. Only with the last election has this finally started to fracture the neoliberal political order with new formations on the left and, very worry- ingly, the extreme right starting to win popular support. This is, of course, a classical feature of social breakdown that is only now, and only in Greece so far, starting to be seen through the course of the post-2008 crisis. These experiences underline the importance of not relegating the democratic movement to a merely auxiliary aspect to socialist transformation, but seeing the two as vitally important parts of a singular process. It is in fact capitalism that treats the political and the economic as separate, formally distinct spheres, precisely in order to foster the 'natural' idea that private property lies outside of democratic control. It is socialists that should want to break down these barriers to democratisation, but to do so we must conceive of socialism as a necessarily democratic project, that will inevitably fail if author- itarianism again triumphs.

For the leadership of Syriza in Greece, a party of the left that is currently surging forward, the test will be whether they can actually break with the logic of liberal democratic political systems today – the "post-democratic" logic. If they can develop new and radical forms of civic, workplace democracy which actually resembles more closely the original democratic ideal of classical Athens and break with the capitalist logic of "represen- tative" power that stands above the people, then this will be a world-changing election. For such actions could start to bring into being a socialist democracy that dismantled capitalist power itself. More likely, unfortunately, is that they will attempt to negotiate new compromises – a new social contract – in conditions where capitalism cannot afford such a settlement and thus in effect succumb to capitalist power. Of course, there are many contingencies, and the emergence of a Latin American style left populist regime in Europe, let alone the danger of reactionary far right forces, and multiple other options, are all possible. But the importance of the Greek events is that it illustrates capitalist realism fractures when society enters a path of breakdown and so it gives us hope for socialist political change emerging out of the crisis.

The fight for democracy cannot be relegated to a secondary issue - it has to be radicalised with a new and modern form of class politics. The organised left is at a disadvantage – imposed on it by the legacy of Stalinism – because in many peoples' minds socialism and democracy are irreconcilable opposites, and that capitalism, despite the problems, at least offers the scope for free individual action. Socialism as the *Erfurt Programme* illustrates had previously promised a radical modernity, to liberate us as humans from oppression and enslavement by elites, but it became synonymous with the very enslavement that it was supposed to be fighting. The possibility of an anticapitalist outcome to the peoples' revolutions of 1989-1991 was aborted precisely because of the strength of this feeling in popular consciousness. Somehow the left must turn this antipodean thinking around.

Indeed, the most extreme forms of antipodean thinking actually appear to be a feature of post-democratic liberalism as political discourse assumes an increasingly irrational character. It is an "upside down world" when Obama can be called a Muslim, a communist, even a fascist on US cable television networks and literally thousands upon thousands of Americans will believe it. A world in which bank bailout measures designed to save US finance capital from ruin are referred to in Congress as "Bolshevism"[106] and where leading British tabloid newspapers refer without apparent irony to Ed Miliband as "Red Ed". It is for the left – and indeed consciousness-transforming movements such as Occupy – to bring these terms back into alignment with their real meanings. Capitalism is actually a great curtailer of choice and freedom. Think about the classical criticism of the Soviet states that they imposed cultural uniformity and it opens up, paradoxically, a critique of neoliberalism, which has imposed a staggering degree of cultural monolithism with icons such as Starbucks and McDonalds lining city-centre avenues in every major metropolis of the world. Such corporations are huge, global institutions that are unaccountable to any form of democratic control. Big blocks of capital such as these impose a certain agenda simply through the threat to sovereign governments that they may take their business elsewhere unless a friendly regulatory agenda will be introduced that is favourable to their own economic expansion. These are profoundly capitalist expressions of a profoundly "post-democratic" world.

The power that the global establishment – operating through highly bureaucratised, technocratic institutions – has over our lives was seen as the Eurozone crisis reached yet another crescendo in the dying months of 2011. Mass popular opposition to austerity in Greece had led Prime Minister Georgios A. Papendreou to attempt to salvage his political career by offering a referendum on the latest austerity measures with a "yes" or "no" question of whether to stay in Europe. It was a cynical move for the question asked of the Greek people would have been a black and white choice: "if you want to stay in the European Union, then you must accept the agony of austerity". But the reaction to it was telling. As international markets tanked, it was an alliance of Angela Merkel and Nicolas Sarkozy that brought down the Greek government, replacing it with a technocratic government of national unity that dropped the question of a popular referendum on the bailout measures. It is as if the crisis is too serious to let ordinary people interfere.

The closer we are to the belly of the beast in the heartlands of western capitalism, the harder it is for us to break their consensus and mount the kind of resistance that can bring down governments on a radical, left wing basis. Without a stronger, unified left the banks will continue to exercise more power over the fate of governments than the people. In this disempowered age, when all we have is a culture of resistance and seemingly no alternative post-capitalist vision, with the left remaining a permanent opposition to the establishment but unable to assert our own agenda, the fight to take control of our lives poses a radical break, a rupture from the status quo. It means democratising every walk of life: the economy, the media, politics, the workplace, unions, strikes, green spaces, parks, sports centres, libraries – we need to assert a politics of universal democratisation. In the words of the *MayDay Manifesto:* "we propose alternatives, because we want to fix the problem... [and move] towards a more democratic world". It is this combination of mass movements pushing for concrete changes in policy while transforming the consciousness of millions of people and raising their horizons to a new kind of politics, which we need to develop.

Indeed, a strong and universal post-capitalist message is needed. In a nutshell it should go something like this: the accumulated detritus of advanced capitalism has to be swept away. We don't want to be appendages of the machines, workers trapped in the hamster wheel, distracted by bread and circuses, while the bread is running out.[107] We will no longer be call centre fodder connected to the matrix by our headsets, with a temp agency taking a third of our salary whilst the bank directors buy another house in the Home Counties. The occupation of the squares is the demand to have a civil society, which is our own, which is not penetrated in a thousand ways by capital and so wedded to a myriad of corporate interest groups. We intend to seize the commons and assert our right to political expression that is not "granted to us" by the powers that be. This is the enduring significance of Occupy and Tahrir: they have created an opening for new forms of radical power.

As the comedian George Carlin has pointed out *"rights aren't 'rights' if someone can take 'em away; they're privileges"*. The fact that in Britain we have only "privileges" that the state can take away when it sees fit is a classic example of the limited democratic fruits the bourgeois revolution has given to the wider mass of the people. Growing popular aversion to these undemocratic limits provides the central opportunity to renew a democratic, socialist project. So if such an anti-authoritarian left is needed, then how does the left need to reorganise politically to develop it? It is this to this question that we shall now turn.

The left: still "betwixt and between"?

In search of strategic thinking

The current political conjuncture for the left was perhaps best summarised by Slavoj Žižek's formula in his address to the Occupy movement in New York: "now the field is open".[108] In a nutshell, Žižek had summarised the basic consequence of the meme-moment that Occupy had realised: it broke the old assumptions, posed huge questions, but did not offer a definitive answer on the politics needed to resolve the social crisis. Now the "way was open" to explore a radical alternative to the status quo that may finally gain a mass hearing.

In any social crisis it is necessary to keep in mind two distinct elements. Firstly, there are the classical features of revolution that have recurred time and again throughout the modern epoch. The polarisation between the left and right, the conservative outlook of the capitalist layers of society amid revolutionary convulsions, and the dramatic "speeding up" of social change, are general features of social crises present to one degree or another in our own period. But, secondly, there is also an immense historical novelty in the current situation; those aspect of crisis which need to be understood in their specificity. One feature of the current moment is the relative durability of the liberal centre *despite* the extent and depth of the social crisis in the West. Only in Greece, so far, have we seen the emergence of a polarisation between the left and right that implies moving beyond neoliberal 'norms'.

In terms of longer-term challenges for the radical left, the new period in world history that was opened by the collapse of the Soviet Union arguably rendered 'all previous bets off'. In the 1980s there were few socialists that factored the possibility of its downfall into their politics, even though they were often defined by their position on 'the Russian question'. It was perhaps understandable that few anticipated the collapse of the USSR, which had after all been a fixture of the global order for decades, but for socialist groupings there was more at stake politically than mere perspective. They were politically defined – i.e. justified their existence as defined ideological currents – largely by their analysis of the Soviet Union, and so its collapse in one way or another shook their assumptions. For this reason, the fall of the Soviet Union should logically open up new avenues for unity and cooperation on the left.

If we take this step to new organisations of the left, then it also becomes possible to work with new layers of activists in order to formulate a radical strategy for today's movements. Activists from Occupy, the student movement, and the new grassroots campaigns in the unions, will often not have a 'conscious programme' in the way that the left understands the term, but they have proven able to build vibrant and exciting campaigns from which we need to learn. Žižek's comments to Occupy are therefore particularly important, because it addressed this issue – 'what politics do we need to win?' – directly to the new layers of resistance who are relatively untouched by past defeats, but still lack a worked-out political strategy. Looking at the question of strategy in these terms means that we do not start with judgements about the irreconcilable nature of the new versus the old left, but try to draw upon a variety of experiences and political traditions to develop effective forms of organisation and radical answers to the capitalist crisis. It is in this spirit that we wrote this book; to try to address, in an open-minded way, "the strategy question". Although we have grounded our standpoint in a longer analysis of some of the challenges of the current situation, we now want to draw out more explicitly our political conclusions.

Talking strategy is all the more important, because the existing projects of the radical left are largely not working. The left remains isolated and itself prone to splits and fragmentation under the pressure of the global capitalist crisis. Against the backdrop of global austerity the situation in Britain is not world changing but is still indicative of wider trends. At the end of 2011 – after twelve months of large-scale mobilisation against austerity starting with the student revolt – the leaders of the biggest public sector union, Unison, led a sell-out of the pension dispute, which had given rise to the first mass strike against the government since it came to power in 2010 and the biggest walkout in decades. That the leadership did not want to carry on the fight is not surprising, but the left was too weak to develop an alternative leadership with real social power at the base. So, despite its protests, it could not restart the action. The result? A defeat.

The problem does not simply come down to strategies of the left, but, because our practices do not exist in a vacuum, we are also affected by the structural and cultural changes that are going on around us. The decline of industrial militancy and the shift to the right in the mainstream politics have all caused ructions on the left; for the sense of isolation creates either a sectarian retrenchment into schemas or the tendency to fall behind the official leaderships – positions we saw during the fall of 2011.

Learning from the past to inform the future
In its own way, this reflects classical problems of the socialist movement, but they are perhaps amplified today due to the isolation and divisions that beset radical politics. It was Rosa Luxemburg who famously summed up the nature of the left's delicate balancing act:

On the one hand, we have the mass; on the other its historic goal, located outside of existing society. On the one hand, we have the day-to-day struggle; on the other, the social revolution. Such are the terms of the dialectical contradiction through which the socialist movement makes its way. It follows that the movement can best advance by tacking betwixt and between the two dangers by which it is constantly being threatened. One is the loss of its mass character; the other, the abandonment of its goal. One is the danger of sinking back to the condition of a sect; the other, the danger of becoming a movement of bourgeois social reform.[109]

Luxemburg would be horrified at where the left, and indeed the socialist project, ended up after her death: the tyranny of Stalinism and the disintegration of the anti-Stalinist left into sects. We have indeed "sunk back into the condition of sects" – not dissimilar to the 19th century where left wing politics was also marked by the existence of a plethora of competing socialist propaganda societies. Now, however, we have to contend with the legacy that Stalinism left for radical political organisation. The Russian Social Democratic Labour Party was, prior to 1917, and in contradistinction to received wisdom, a relatively plural, democratic organisation that had lively, open political inter-change and debate with other factions within the labour and progressive movement. But this democratic heritage was lost in the 1920s and 1930s, because a top-down and bureaucratic model of political organisation displaced it. In the post-war period the radical left, not universally, but largely, tended to replicate the more negative aspects of "vanguardism". Not the unobjec-tionable idea that once one takes up radical socialist ideas we should try to bring others behind these ideas and give leadership to the movement, but the tendency to subordinate mass movements to the narrow organisational interests of the Leninist sect. In part, this reflects a way that these groups came to conceive their relationship to the class as lonely "torch-bearers" of truth. Morris Stein summed up this outlook in 1944 at convention of the Socialist Workers Party (US):

We are monopolists in the field of politics. We can't stand any competition. We can tolerate no rivals. The working class, to make the revolution can do it only through one party and one program. This is the lesson of the Russian Revolution. That is the lesson of all history since the October Revolution. Isn't that a fact? This is why we are out to destroy every single party in the field that makes any pretence of being a working-class revolutionary party. Ours is the only correct program that can lead to revolution. Everything else is deception, treachery. We are monopolists in politics and we operate like monopolists.[110]

That this appalling caricature of Marxist political organisation was expressed within a grouping that was fighting Stalinism in the labour movement underlines the extent to which the wrong and reactionary assumptions that Stalin had fostered came to be absorbed across the movement. Internal regimes of socialist groupings also, it has to be said, continue to tend towards a bureaucracy and top-down forms of decision making and at the most extreme even forbid members from expressing disagreements with party lines in public. These assumptions have done immense damage to the socialist movement and they are entrenched practices that will take time to overcome and transcend. A starting point needs to be a recognition of the importance of plurality, which sees the legitimacy of opposing viewpoints in the formulation of Marxism, and the forms of organisation that grant substantial autonomy and democratic control to base organisations, as well as encouraging full and open debate on political strategy.

Today's left is often caught "betwixt and between" in the following way. We rightly see the need to strike the widest possible unity in the labour movement for immediate reforms, but the overall character of the movement is increasingly "post-socialistic". Consider how at the TUC demonstration in Britain, the official message was "march for the alternative", but the alternative was not anti-systemic, was not *socialist*, but limited to highly partial calls for tackling tax heavens, introducing a Tobin Tax, and investing in jobs. Often social movements, even those headed by more radical forces way to the left of official leaderships, will campaign for measures that are consciously limited to such reforms. There is normally little in the way of robust and intelligent criticism of the official leaderships, or anticapitalist agitation that has a "meme appeal" beyond the usual abstract socialist propaganda.

No one can honestly promise to pull a "socialist movement" like the one Luxemburg knew out of thin air, but we do need to reflect upon what such a movement would look like in the 21st century, for it is unlikely to simply repeat the language and aesthetic of the German social democracy. Would it not look a lot like Occupy – a movement that drew in unions, which took direct action, promoted an anticapitalist message, and had a wide, sweeping popular appeal? If these new movements are considered in these terms, then we can start to think creatively about the lessons drawn from the past so that Occupy might move in the direction of instilling socialist consciousness in far wider layers of working class people.

The contemporary crisis of the left is therefore both chronic and acute. The chronic problem remains the isolation of revolutionary socialists in the post war world and their decline into the sect form. The acute problem is the immediate inability to lead the resistance necessary to turn the tables on austerity and provide working class people with confidence and belief in the socialist project. In times of capitalist crisis these fault lines continually threaten to widen and deepen under the pressure of events. And they won't be easily overcome.

The problem of reformist leadership has its origins in the transformation that took place within the socialist movement of Rosa Luxemburg's time. It was symbolised by the support the social democratic parties of the Second International had given to their respective countries during the First World War and further consolidated as these same parties became crucial pillars of social stability for capital within the working class movement in the decades thereafter. This development powerfully confirmed Luxemburg's famous claim that those who advocated the path of social reform over revolution were not in fact proposing a different route to the same goal but had a different goal entirely: a moderated capitalism rather than a fundamental transformation away from it towards socialism.[111] It is important to see the contemporary isolation of the left within this context; it was the march rightwards by mass parties of the working class that condemned the left to the fringes and a return to the "sect form" through which it had existed prior to the Second International. Whatever criticisms we might have of how the left has *grown use to* and *de facto accepted as inevitable* this existence, we must nonetheless recognise these historical circumstances.

Neither is our current state merely a logical consequence of taking the "reformist road" but reflects the transformations we saw in the 20th century – the emergence of mass consumer culture, the strengthening of individual rights and freedoms in the West, the relative denial of these aspirations in the East, and the consequent discrediting of socialism – have all affected what the working class has come to expect from its leaders, indeed, what they *want* from politics. The "what's in it for me" culture that emerged in the 1960s of consumer expansion was initially favourable to the unions, or at least it proved to be in Britain, because union power was seen as key to securing growing material prosperity. But Thatcher was able to capitalise on disenchantment with strikes in the late 1970s, laying the way for neoliberalism to break the unions, and consequently it was the politics of social mobility (and inequality) that increasingly trumped the politics of class struggle resistance.

All of this impacted on the fortunes of the radical left, but in the instability caused by the breakdown of the social compromise that marked the post-war boom there was nonetheless a long period of powerful ascent and opportunity. The radical left parties today that stand above the others in terms of size trace their origins to the post-1968 radicalisation.

The onset of structural problems in the economy ("stagflation" as it was known in Britain), growing labour movement discontent and the new social movements, allowed relatively small groupings of communists to increase in size considerably; from hundreds and then later to thousands. It is easy to look back at this period of growth now and see it as puzzling given the general decline of socialism across the 20th century. If we read history as a series of inevitable occurrences that somehow could be known in advance, then drawing this viewpoint might be permissible. But the post-1968 left success-fully fostered the belief that the decline of capitalism in the West and the stagnation and crises of Stalinism in the East were opening up a sea of global contradictions out of which a healthy revolutionary Marxism would emerge as a mass force. This was actually not an entirely unrealistic perspective given the tectonic social struggles seen across the East and the West after 1968, but it would always be a challenge given that growing disillu-sionment with *communism* and class struggle politics per se, not *merely Stalinism*, was becoming a feature of global politics in the 1980s.

In the mid-1970s the Trotskyist movement, although badly fragmented and in the process of creating sects that would ultimately become highly ossified in their worldview, nonetheless had a certain confidence of being on the right side of history "this time round". Yet, it was not the revolutionary left who would emerge out of the social conflicts of the 1970s and 1980s across the globe, with a strong claim to have anticipated the actual course of development. Of the tendencies within the left who could claim to have acted as "prophets" for a triumphant neoliberal revolution it was the eurocommunists that argued from an early stage that neoliberalism was creating a new hegemony based on individualism and social mobility and so appeared to understand more closely the meaning of Thatcherism. While this should not excuse the passivity and retreat they advocated in the face of neoliberalism – which played a similar role at the political level to business unionism at the economic level – they did capture something about Thatcher's appeal that was overlooked on the rest of the left. Namely, that it accorded with the desire for individual rights and expression – albeit in a crude and distorted, indeed selfish, form – of the post 1968 generation. The desire for individual freedom is something that is still with us – a feature of how people have come to understand their relationship with one another and often with politics. It is an important factor in the inability of cadre Leninist parties to make a substantial breakthrough, because their model of organisation, which sadly forgets the relatively loose and open structure of the Russian social democracy during the periods of legality under Tsarism, does not chime with the cultural desire for individuality. If there is a lesson to draw and reflect on in the eurocommunist understanding of Thatcher, it is that the left has rediscover the aspect of the socialist tradition that championed freedom of expression and individual rights, rather than simply see such discourses as existing in a crude counter-position to the socialist collective.

Historically, this would have helped appeal to broader layers of the working class in the West, because it would have cut *with the grain* of cultural transformations in how freedom was increasingly conceived within these societies. Still, this reality did not make the more widely held general prognosis of the left, which, as Anderson expressed, saw the crises of the 1970s and 1980s as representing an opportunity to rebuild the working class movement on the lines of anti-Stalinist socialism, at all farfetched. World changing events gave rise to resistance on a quite revolutionary scale, from huge labour movement protests and strikes in the West to revolutions in the East. But no hegemonic, anti-Stalinist left politics emerged.

The competing projects of the left remained hampered by disunity across this period. It undermined the extent to which they could present radical left wing politics as a *credible* alternative to neoliberalism, Stalinism and social democracy, in a similar manner to the ineffectiveness of the contemporary radical left. Indeed, the rise of the post-1968 left was a time of ideological flux and procreation of new outlooks – Maoism, a myriad of Trotskyist fragments, third world nationalism, Guevaraism, Autonomism, and the new identity politics. This fragmentation was probably inevitable – and certainly it would not have been possible politically to simply "unite" these disparate ideologies – but the disunity amongst the serious Marxists, such as the Trotskyists of Anderson's generation, was certainly damaging.

While the core of activists around Trotsky thought of themselves as the only consistently revolutionary force on the planet in the 1930s, by the 1950s the inheritors of this tradition had largely slipped into an accommodation with Stalinism, albeit in difficult conditions that Trotsky himself did not anticipate, and became increasingly fractured in the face of global challenges and developments. The resulting fragmentation of Trotskyism is not a happy story. It constructed a "thousand and one" ossified, closed, often simply crude and "wrong" new orthodoxies all incarnated in and defended by a myriad of left propaganda societies, large and small. Unity projects were attempted, but these too often succumbed to "get rich quick" opportunism as apparently the only way out of sect isolation. Indeed, the Trotskyist movement tended to respond opportunistically to the rising tide of third world nationalism and the emergence of superficially "anti-Stalinist" Stalinism such as the various forms symbolised by the figures of Mao, Che, Castro, and Tito. For instance, in response to the Nicaraguan Revolution in the 1980s, the Trotskyist Fourth International embarked on a series of disastrous unity projects with small heterogeneous groupings of supporters of the Sandinistas. Lacking the sufficient agreement needed to keep such parties together they collapsed as these currents responded in diverse ways to the pressure of events.

A similar problem would have been confronted had unity initiatives been undertaken over the last decade that attempted to unite small bands of supporters of Hugo Chavez's "Bolivarian Revolution". It underlines the importance of having a sufficient degree of political agreement around which unity can be genuinely organic rather than merely formal and so inevitably unstable. The question, though, is whether forms of organisation can be found that allow different programmes and strategies to co-exist within the same party, and within certain parameters of common agreement on the action that is necessary for the collective to take. Seen in these terms, the fragmentation of the revolutionary Marxist movement is particularly damaging and less justified politically. Indeed, the proliferation of new narrowly conceived orthodoxies is something that particularly beset the Trotskyist movement as each sect laid claim to the "genuine heritage" of Trotsky's international. The fact so many of these positions were defined in relation to the "Russian question" makes the continued organisational divisions of the left all the more problematic given the Soviet Union no longer exists. If we are to overcome disunity in the decades ahead, socialists who want to more beyond the "sect model" of political work, i.e. those who reject the practice that sees the growth and development of the organisation as an end in itself regardless of the working class struggle will need to regroup and find new avenues for unity.

Weakness and isolation alone necessitates taking this step. But as the Marxist writer and activist Stathis Kouvelakis has argued we can at least take comfort in the fact that the crisis offers up the opportunity to destabilise the received wisdoms of the radical left:

A properly historical and materialist, that is to say a Marxist, understanding of Marxism itself shows that each major crisis of capitalism destabilises Marxism, both in its cognitive coordinates and in its practical, political dimension, forcing it to reinvent itself as it does with capitalism.[112]

De-stabilisation of the conceptual coordinate of Marxism occurs due to the multiple spheres through which a crisis reverberates; from the economic, to social, cultural, ideological, political, even geographical and environmental. Each of these terrains adds their own determinations to the instability of human evolution and requires a reformulation of conceptual categories to make sense of contemporary developments. But this process of crisis is far from always positive and healthy. Kouvelakis notes how the crisis of the 1930s was enormously disruptive to the collective psychology of the socialist movement and is remembered not as a period of breakthrough, but a time of quite harrowing defeats; from the annihilation of the German workers' movement to the consolidation of Soviet Stalinization in the Great Purges. This alone illustrates how there is no axiomatic relationship between a social crisis and a renewed, reinvigorated radical left. But the contrast between the 1930s and our current epoch is nonetheless enormous. For what made the defeats of socialism in the 1930s at the hands of Hitler, Stalin, Franco, and others, so destabilising was they struck the movement down at a high point of apparently ineluctable ascent. Our crisis will inevitably destabilise the left, but the fact that it does so from a point of chronic weakness means that the form it takes will be radically different from the 1930s. Even though one of the problems of the disintegration of the left into the "sect form" is that small groups can become apparently immune from the crisis as they draw on self-justificatory orthodoxies, it is still nonetheless the case that the challenge the crisis represents does create an important impetus for change. Here the imperative starts not from the standpoint of a relatively conscious socialist movement led through two decades of defeat as in the 1930s, but, the hope is that new avenues exist for the creation of such a movement afresh, which, in turn creates a powerful pressures for unity.

The change we seek should not only be limited to finding new avenues to overcome disunity, but also starting to develop strategies that are simultaneously able to disrupt capital and appear to represent a *credible* alternative to the system. If left unity is one dimension to this credibility, the other is being able to articulate a strategy that is both revolutionary and *concrete* – no easy thing.

Indeed, the decline of the left has had serious implications for our ability to be taken seriously as a genuine force, one which can achieve tangible gains in politics. In his recent book, *First as Tragedy then as Farce*, Žižek laments the fate of the left as permanent but "loyal" opposition to reaction. Unable to win we can only take comfort in being "right":

> In a famous confrontation at the university of Salamanca in 1936, Miguel de Unamuno quipped at the Francoists: "Vencereis, pero no convencereis" ("You will win, but you will not convince") – is this all that today's Left can say to triumphant global capitalism? Is the Left predestined to continue to play the role of those who... convince but nevertheless still lose (and are especially convincing in retroactively explaining... their own failure)?[113]

Can we, left activists, really fault this philosopher's assessment? Hardly. It speaks powerfully to the long-term decline of the left under the hammer blows of defeat. But it also identifies the practices of the left that reflect this legacy: permanent oppositionism – i.e. getting lost in focusing exclusively on building day-to-day resistance, and forgetting the vital need to develop a credible, positive perspective for socialist transformation that strikes a chord.

Can we develop a concrete strategy? Similar themes have been picked up by Kouvelakis who has argued that a problem arises out of isolation that impact upon how the left has come to generally conceive of the relationship between its overall goals and the immediate imperatives of social struggle. It should be noted that this again returns to the "betwixt and between" dilemma originally posed by Rosa Luxemburg. Kouvelakis, in a manner similar to our own concerns here, focuses on the dissonance between aspects of the political message of the left and its ability to actualise it in credible and meaningful ways. Take, for example, the slogan "we won't pay for their crisis" – it assumes that the argument inside the working class has actually already *been won*, as Kouvelakis argues:

>...The problem with the slogan "We won't pay for their crisis" is that its performative dimension ("We won't pay") presupposes that our objective has already been achieved, which means that a sufficient number of people are convinced that there are other ways to deal with the crisis than those currently on offer, and that they are convinced about this alternative possibility in a situation where action is needed immediately, otherwise it wouldn't be a situation of crisis.[211]

The danger is that such formulas ("we won't pay") become not appeals whose aspirational quality is designed to inspire, but lose meaning as the left fails to persuade workers *not to pay*. In short, to actually render a left wing challenge *credible* a far more concrete strategy has to be articulated. The message of the left is often, however, stuck between minimal demands – in particular opposing the latest austerity attack of capital on working people, "no cuts", etc. – and excessive generality in its appeals to socialism. A particular problem, Kouvelakis argues, in countries such as Ireland and Greece that have experienced extreme levels of austerity, is that the left tends to mimic what he called "syndi-calist or trade union" forms of agitation. The left enters into a cycle of social mobilisation around demands like "strike to defend pensions", only to then find that these were basically ineffective to confront the *political* imposition of a generalised attack on the public sector. In the face of such a political offensive, then a *credible political response* is required that can reach out not only to public sector workers on the frontline, but also working class service users, young people, students and the unemployed. To speak of "credibility" in this way is not to say that we should simply parrot reformist answers to the crisis. Indeed, Kouvelakis also noted how the reformist wing of the anti-neoliberal left, for example, Attac in France, or the European Left Party, persisted for some time after 2008 in continuing to put forward a reform perspective for the European Union, which was rightly perceived by millions of workers as an unrealistic vision of social change. For the radical left, the challenge is to find demands and policies that are able to move beyond this practice marked by "propagandistic attitudes", on the one hand, the familiar appeals to socialism, and "trade union agitation" on the other.

A further problem is that the form "trade union agitation" takes can often fall behind the strategies of the existing leader-ships of the working class. Often this is justified in terms of appealing to the lower levels of confidence in the working class movement – the logical idea that through struggle workers will develop greater belief in their power and thus more likely to fight – and, while there is some truth in this, it ignores the fact that the problem of confidence actually arises from an anterior difficulty: workers' collective feeling of being disempowered. Union bureaucracies cultivate this, not always through conscious design, but by creating hierarchies in which the full time, paid officialdom reside in offices far removed from the daily grind of workplace organisation at the base of the unions. The decline of the left exists in reciprocal relationship to the decline of the grassroots unionism, because bureaucracies do not put resources into cultivating active workplace organisation that could stimulate a resurgent class struggle politics and the left does not have the social strength with which it can direct its energies into reenergising these layers. Consequently, workers do not have the grassroots organisations extending across a sector that could give them an alternative centre of power to the official hierarchies in the union movement. The loss of the idea that workers should take direct actions regardless of whether it is acceptable to their leaders is also a feature of Britain's anti-union legislation. They make 'wildcat strikes' illegal, so just walking off the job because your workmate has been sacked or management that morning announced 50 redundancies is prohibited by law. Every strike must be formally balloted and officially approved by the union and the courts, which, in turn, furthers the bureaucratisation of the unions due to the enormous administrative apparatuses that are required in order to meet the legal requirements for balloting. Spontaneous grassroots activism has had an anchor hung around its neck. The lack of grassroots institutions outside of the official structures exacerbates this problem. The anticuts movement exhibits this similar problem of collective disempowerment because the centre of power that drives the cuts and austerity seems far too remote, too far removed from our ordinary lives; what can we do when the problem is massive international banks and the European Union bosses?

The problem is thus not simply confidence; it is *self*-confidence. Do you have a sense that you can do-it-yourself, that you can take action even when the union structures or the official leaders do not? Confidence in the movement or the union as a whole is often misplaced. Every movement or union is made up of potentially antagonistic forces, fault lines are built into them from the start, for instance between the members and the leaders. Unless individuals feel empowered, not just confident, to stand up for what they feel is right and take action despite the potential witch hunt from the union headquarters or persecution by management, then we are stuck in a vicious circle of defeat.

Last year electricians ("Sparks") across Britain organised in a spirited grassroots mobilisation that was a worked example of the kinds of movement that can unseat the official hierarchies of the labour movement. They knew the attack was coming on their industrial agreements, some militants called a conference (a prominent member of whom is in a socialist organisation), they elected a steering committee, organised a plan of weekly protests across the country and demanded the union to call a ballot. The slowness of the union in backing them up and giving them the tools they need to take action is indicative of the problem that the official structures are unresponsive to grassroots mobilisations coming from below. When workers backs are to the wall then the idea of a rank and file initiative can have real resonance. The confidence of the sparks to take action was greatly improved because activists developed the organisation to do it. It is why we have now seen wildcat actions across the country with over a thousand electricians taking unofficial action. Compared to other sectors like health or education workers, the electricians are streets ahead in terms of combativity.

When the issue is posed in this way, then confidence is just one factor amongst many. Perhaps the lack of confidence is most acute on the activist left, because we tend to *read* our own doubt into the working class, when we should be developing spirited organisations from the base that can engender the self-confidence workers need to fight to win. The task facing us now, which is posed acutely by the scale of the crisis and the inability of our unions to rise to that challenge, is to build a strong grassroots' movements which can empower the workers to take more radical action. This means effective leadership not just solidarity.

Thinking about how we win means that we have to come back to the challenge Lloyd George posed to the leaders of the Triple

Alliance in 1919. It is necessary to unleash the full social weight of the unions - mass all out strikes and huge protests and occupations – drawing in workers, organised and unorganised, for action. Everything else is a protest strike or a stage managed confrontation. But once posed in these terms, it shows how we need to build organisations that break with capitalist realist assumptions: that are, in short, actually prepared to force a political crisis of neoliberalism. The union leaders in 1919 were beaten because *they could have won*. The real paradox of effective unionism in the capitalist realist world is that we have not mobilised the kind of radical working class that Lloyd George was referring to, but the leaderships of the unions are still conscious of the stark choice any workers' mobilisation poses; the status quo and an easy, privileged life or a decisive conflict. Partly this reflects the privileged life of bureaucratic layers, but it also underlines the ways in which the all-encompassing nature of capitalist realist ideology is unseated even when only partially punctuated. Just as the election of Ed Miliband led the ludicrous charge he was "red", so too did the mobilisation of workers in the pensions' dispute last year lead the right wing media to proclaim a return of industrial discontent and a decisive conflict between the unions and the Tories, even though the strike action did not go beyond a protest. Union leaders tend to go out of their way to emphasise they are not confronting capital and this feeds into the timid forms of resistance that they advocate to protest against the system.

Only if we think in radical political terms – about breaking out of the logic of capitalist realism and imagining an entirely different system – will we take the path of real resistance. That's why the solution cannot be simply economic or industrial, undermining capitalism realism requires of us that we act and think politically about social movements, and that we seek to transform trade unions into fighting organisations on an overly political basis. If we keep this in mind, we can help develop a credible political alternative and thus bridge the often all too often gapping gap between the socialist vision and our practical agitation.

The dangers of mere "syndicalist agitation" also pose a challenge to how we actually conceive of the day-to-day trade union work activists undertake: what is its purpose and role within a wider project of socialist transformation? Once you understand the dangers of an exclusive focus on trade union-like mobilisation, we do not just have to think politically but we also have to think about our trade union activity in political terms.

In a situation of capitalist realism – where a credible anticapitalism appears so, so elusive from the daily grind of life under neoliberalism – those on the left who want to ignore the question of an alternative, or put it across with the same tired and propagandistic formulas that are incapable of reaching out to new layers, are simply articulating a failed logic. The "prefigurative" dimension to Occupy – the idea that it is trying to organise in a way that is reflective of the goals that it is seeking to achieve – is often scorned by the radical left. But this horizontalism plainly has communist implications[114] and is an attempt at developing an anti-authoritarian anticapitalism that does not collapse into the tyrannies of the past. Too often socialists, or specifically, advocates of the distorted notion of "Leninism" that became normalised in the 20th century, scorn this and draw sharp distinctions between the centralised and "top down" method of organisation we advocate today and the horizontal nature of the future communist society. After the defeats of the last century we need to ask whether such assumptions are at all credible; are they not damaging to our project? The American radical writer, Pham Binh, has combined his personal experience of Occupy with a re-reading of the pre-1917 Bolshevik tradition, to emphasise the plurality, autonomy and democratic ethos of the Russian party prior to the bureaucratic degeneration of the revolution. This re-conceptualisation of what "Leninism" means should also soften criticism of "prefigurative" methods of organisation that seek to imbue movements with an ethos that is worthy of the ideals of a truly equal, classless stage of human development.

The merits of this approach are twofold. Firstly, it can help us develop anti-authoritarian forms of authority that rearticulate the socialist project in credible, democratic terms. Finding a balance between effective authority, co-ordination, and participatory and plural forms of organisation will be important in this regard. On both the sect-building left and amongst the new horizontalists of the social movement there is a shared propensity to what David Harvey calls, "an all-consuming fetishism of organisational form" in which "programmatic principles are dogmatically articulated... as if no alternative form would ever be necessary or valuable".[116] He notes how the anarcho-libertarian, Murray Bookchin, has promoted confederalism as a programme for direct democracy in which communes are formed defined according territories, such as the modern urban cities, but then – due to the nature of modern social development – have to co-ordinate the use of resources through non-hierarchical networks of administration. Although this implicitly acknowledges the problem that mass society poses for a programme of *pure horizontalism,* Harvey argues, correctly in our view, it is still insufficient, because some form of democratic authority has to exist above the local commune in order to manage any conflicts over resources. But, the point nonetheless, is that these differences of programme have to be assessed according to the practical conditions of modern human life, debated freely in collaborative forums for the renewal left wing politics, in a way that helps us transcend the fractured nature of the left.

Secondly, and no less politically, we need to draw into social struggle those who are not attracted to the traditional methods and aesthetic of the left by developing vibrant spaces for artistic and cultural reproduction. Studies have shown in Britain how the young people who rioted in August 2011 were highly politically, particularly in terms of racism and their understanding of the daily injustices of police violence and repression.[117] But none of these young people had been drawn behind the positive project of the radical left and paid a tragically high cost for the riots of that summer. Music and modern culture are defining political reference points for this generation, but they are often absent from the daily practice of the political left, whose cultural reference points can often appear anachronistic. If the prefigurative dimension of protest is to be useful beyond the circles of activists attracted to its ideals hitherto, then it will have to become radically more popular and imagine visions of life after capitalism that these working class youth can relate to.

The decline of popular aspirations for socialism and the expansion of liberal hegemony globally has inevitably impacted on the form resistance to the system has taken. One of the most important counter-hegemonic movements of the last ten years has been the World Social Forum, a huge gathering of some 150,000 participants that originated in Brazil but spread outwards to become a global movement as part of the upsurge of discontent with neoliberal globalisation. In the WSF forums, the "old ideologies" of the Marxist left were all very much present. Yet, the dominate discourse at the event and the multiples numbers of appeals that came out of it, did not really broach an anticapitalist politics as such, but tended to advocate altermondialism ("alternative globalisation"), that is, a shift from neoliberalism towards a new social contract that involved the protection of the public space from capital. Globally this did not achieve influence at the level of state politics except in Latin America; from the moderated neoliberalism of Lula to the more traditional left populism of Huge Chavez – neither of which could be reasonably seen in anticapitalist terms. While much of the left globally embraced the Bolivarian project as an alternative to neoliberalism, its distinctiveness simply lay in the fact that so few states globally still had the view that a degree of state planning is important to the healthy functioning of a market economy. Even though his social programmes drew upon the country's oil wealth it was the state capitalist model that made it distinctive. In 2005, at the WSF, Hugo Chavez was the star of the show as Latin America's most radical figure, but in subsequent years the emergence of a new "Boligarchy", coalesced around banking and financial wealth with ties to the regime, silenced many of these excited voices.[118] Even though this did not represent a credible anticapitalist vision the fact it appeared to partially punctuate global neoliberal hegemony underlines what Mark Fisher says about the seemingly all-pervasive nature of capitalist realism representing its central Achilles' heel.[119] Even only partial ruptures appear to badly displace the old assumptions underpinning the global political order. But for the radical left – whose project is to *actually transcend and not merely superficially obstruct* – being conscious of such "false dawns" is crucial if we are to avoid dead ends.

In the World and European Social Forum, the disjuncture between propagandistic attitudes and syndicalist agitation was again a central problematic for the Marxist left. The calls that came out of its assemblies very much fell into the category of "syndicalist agitation" – albeit at times a highly effective and powerful form of it. The most dramatic statement was the appeal of the Assembly of Social Movements at the Florence European Social Forum for a global day of action against the Iraq war that culminated in the huge demonstrations of February 15 2003. For us, this day of action remains one of the most defining and extraordinary moments of our political activism. In London, over a million people came onto the street, matched in a plethora of other cities, and exceeded in Rome, where 3 million people participated in the biggest anti-war protest ever known. Despite the enormous instability of the post-2008 world no social uprisings have matched the scale of protest seen globally at the beginning of this century in the anti-war and anticapitalist movements. There was a hope and optimism that defined these protests and the ethos of the left, that in the new, much more bitter and testing terrain of the global economic crisis we are yet to match. Even Occupy, which was inspirational and highly "forward looking" in its ethos, did not create the same impression that the anticapitalist movement did *in some countries* (never in Britain, incidentally) that the left stood on the cusp of actually changing society dramatically. That this belief pervaded the anticapitalist movement, or at least it did so for a period, was arguably part of its success, for it drew on the sociological power of collective belief, i.e. the simple fact that individuals are more likely to fight when they think they will win.

The radical Marxist left were some of the most vocal advocates of the global anti-war protest on February 15 2003 in the assembly meetings, but you would not have known it because they struggled to differentiate themselves from the multiple ideological currents present. Partly this was due to the undemocratic rules of the social forum that banned the *open and formal* participation of political parties which merely resulted in leading political figures, even Lula and Chavez themselves, absurdly participating as "individuals" within the forum. The rules were in theory designed to uphold plurality and emphasise the "social movement" character of the event, but they reproduced within the movement some of the most central "post-political" assumptions of capitalist realism. Given the high profile political *individuals* like Chavez had within the event, they also helped solidify the hegemony of *altermondialism* over more anticapitalist alternatives. But the radical left largely failed to formulate credible political strategies that went beyond the calls to action ("syndicalist agitation") of the social forum assemblies, while inside the movement their intervention was highly propagandistic: numerous seminars debating Marxism versus Autonomism and so on coupled with the usual aesthetic and cultural form of "party intervention". Consequently, within the assemblies where action was organised they were *invisible*, but when they were in the walls of these huge forums they were sometimes *so visible* they appeared as outsiders intervening into the movement rather than as insider participants. In a sense, this reflected an age old problem of the disjuncture between theory and practice within radical left wing politics. After numerous seminars it still wasn't clear how the classical Marxist critique of the Autonomism of Hardt and Negri actually impacted *practical political choices*. Mediation between effective theory and effective practice largely occluded the party-building left.

Finding organisational forms that provide sufficient unity so that we can present a credible challenge to the system and sufficient elasticity to allow both divergent programmes to *co-exist* and be mediated *into practice*, is the central strategic question for the left. While in recent years, particularly in the context of the Latin American left and the rise of the social forum movement, there has been much discussion of a "return of strategy" – i.e. of strategic, power-orientated left wing politics – the extent of this can be questioned.

The term was coined by the recently deceased leader of the New Anticapitalist Party in France, Daniel Bensaïd, who argued that in the context of the Chávez regime, which was at that time in a left wing phase, the idea of taking power and installing radical anticapitalist governments backed up by popular movements on the streets and in the workplaces had undergone strategic renewal. But, conscious of the damage that participation of Trotskyists in Lula's capitalist government had caused, he urged caution without entirely ruling out joining such coalitions in certain circumstances.[120] This was seen as a corrective to the anti-political ideas of John Holloway, one time popular figure in the anticapitalist movement, who famously argued for a strategy to "change the world without taking power", and represented a renewed confidence of the left that the question of power was opening up again. But the decline in the radicalism of Latin American left populism undermined Bensaïd's view.

Moreover, even leaving to one side the principles of Bensaïd's position, the proposition there has been a "return of strategy" along the lines he suggested is debateable. If we think of the radical strategies of the 1960s and 1970s there were at least three perspectives which in their own way commanded significant influence amongst wider layers of people: the cumulative transformation of society through the gradual colonisation of the liberal democratic state by the reformist left; the insurrectionary peasant war of the Chinese Revolution that later inspired numerous global uprisings; and the seizure of power by urban-based sovietic bodies of the working class *a la* the Russian Revolution. Each of these strategies retains supporters and a certain appeal, but none of them have been able to break the spell of capitalist realism by appearing to offer a credible and realistic road for the left.

We cannot approach anticapitalist strategy today without acknowledging that we have been through nearly two centuries of anticapitalism that have produced an enormous variety of strategic outlooks and experiences. We are not starting, therefore, from a blank slate and we cannot hope for some kind of clean break with the past even if it was desirable, but a messy and difficult period of flux and uncertainty in our strategic designs and aspirations.

History never repeats itself exactly, but the disparate forces that came together to form the First International – from Marxists, to utopian socialists, anarchists or trade unionists – confronted a similar challenge of grouping together diverse layers in a common project. Socialist sects, trade unions, radical democrats, anarchists and assorted intellectuals make up the current forces of the left - no one group can be considered completely hegemonic and each current brings to the table certain strengths and weaknesses. A drive for unity can help create a sense of renewed purpose, that we can build something which may involve organisational compromise, but agreement on the key tasks facing us today. The left we need to build is of a new type, one that is as critical of itself as it is of capitalism, one that confronts problems head on and demands more of itself and its traditions. It is a left which is as committed to changing itself, its practice and its outlook, as well as the world around us.

In this context, we have to make the case for plural organisations of the left with many tendencies and platforms of various political colourations. Ultimately we need effective anticapitalist organisation that come to be recognised as a serious threat to the ruling class, which can act as a real leadership within the social movements, not by imposition but by a genuine unity of interests between revolutionaries and the people. Of course, this cannot be created by declaration. It will require a fundamental realignment of the left which will take time to organise and make happen, but is slowly occurring under the pressure of events.

Plurality brings with it the danger they try to unite mutually opposed tendencies, which give a new project an inherent instability, but, while being conscious of this, we must also recognise the benefits of building common groupings. Socialist propaganda groups suffer from a lack of communication amongst them and often interact only by way of conflict rather than trying to cultivate a common method of working, and this tends to negate the possibility of sharing knowledge, experience and developing common analyses. Developing organisations that allow different viewpoints to cross-fertilise builds trust, solidarity and makes possible the development of a common outlook and position on the tasks we face.

A more radical argument can be made around this point. If socialists still take their preferred "ideal type" model of organisation to be the Bolsheviks in Russia at the dawn of the last century, then they need to consider the journey of common experience that those revolutionaries went through to create the organisation that "made the revolution". The Bolsheviks were a product of trial and error, splits and fusions, debates and regular political upheavals both within their faction-come-party and the conflicts in the labour movement.

Of course, there were certain principles and programmatic points that emerged overtime, but they did so in the course of common struggle and collective debate. The left tends to take the end point of this experience, "Bolshevism", as its starting point and this tends to exclude the process of development an organisation has to go to become such a mass party.

History, in any case, needs to inform our practice without dictating it. In many respects, the Bolsheviks inhabited a quite different world to our own. If we think about how many times capitalism has reinvented itself in light of new challenges, if we look also at the cumulative transformations of socialist thought across the 20th century, then we have a wealth of paradigms and outlooks on which we can draw to try to formulate a credible left wing politics. We should not try to retrace the steps of past revolutionaries any more than we should forget to draw upon the lessons of the Russian Revolution for our own times.

A practice-informed socialist politics is one that can capture the spirit of the times, can outline the concrete steps that we need to take in the here and now. It must avoid the mistake, all too common in orthodox Marxism, of becoming prisoners of the past and so inverting what should be a fundamentally *progressive* – in the sense of forward looking – worldview into a backward looking dogma that fails to appreciate the novelty of our times.

The future of the radical left

We earlier referred, following Gramsci, to the current conjuncture in world politics as an "organic crisis". This means it is not a "normal" recession, but a crisis that extends deep into the social fabric of society, which has multiple ideological, cultural, environmental, and geographical dimensions, and compels political actors to "find solutions" to it politically and economically. There are two particular dimensions to the crisis that are worth emphasising. The first is its potential geopolitical fallout as the institutions of the 1945 settlement have to adapt to the growing political and economic power of states such as China, India and Brazil. The second lies in the threat to the improved living standards of workers in the West, which were won during the post-war boom of the 1950s and 1960s. These so-called "privileges" are increasingly under pressure as they render economies uncompetitive in the globalised world. There is a real danger of a new wave of historical defeats of the working class, but also very real opportunities for the unions to turn the tables on capital as one cog within an upsurge in "subaltern" mobilisation.

Facing these challenges a revivified revolutionary politics has to break from its various prevalent incarnations that have grown content in one way or another with isolation. We need to take advantage of the antagonisms of the current social crisis to build and renew forms of dynamics of struggle that can deepen the cracks in the capitalist order.

Will a new left have to clarify its strategy at the level of principle? Certainly it should. A new radical politics should be opposed to all discrimination, be clear in its opposition to war and imperialism, take every opportunity to develop grassroots "bottom up" organising in the labour movement, be trenchantly opposed to the reformist bureaucracies in the unions, be clear that a fundamental, socialist alternative is needed in place of capitalism, fight to empower working class people at every level of society, from the workplace to the community, and advocate bold tactics such as the indefinite strike and occupations. But it must also take care not to simply create afresh the kind of closed orthodoxies, embodied in a "fixed" organisational form and based on a narrowly conceived ideological tradition, which came to undermine the living renewal of a pluralistic Marxism in the post-war period. We do not want a fixed dogma that is simply recapitulated, but rather a Marxism seen as a set of ideas in need of creative re-elaboration, with a great deal of flexibility in tactics, pedagogy in language and drawing on a variety of new cultural reference points. We need to focus on building the kinds of relationships with new layers that can help make socialist ideas hegemonic again in the minds, outlook and practice of the working class movement.

We also need to think hard about the lessons of the last ten years – not merely those we can draw from the recent rise of protest in the economic crisis, but also the radicalisation we saw at the dawn of the century in the global wave of anticapitalist protest. This punctuated, but only partially and monetarily, many of the assumptions of the post-1989 world.

Considering the significance of these protests for the renewal and redevelopment of the radical left back in 2001, Alex Callinicos said: "Since Seattle the revolutionary left has been embarking – along with many others, fortunately – on a new voyage. There is no map to guide us—no set of rules or obvious historical reference point to dictate what we should do. The potential rewards are enormous. History will not forgive us if we miss this chance."[121] The question of whether our current voyage is the same as the one that the left began in Seattle, 1999, can be answered in both the affirmative and the negative. Protests after Seattle did bring into radical politics many activists, like ourselves, who have persisted with trying to build and develop a fundamental alternative to capitalism. They also succeeded in shaking the optimistic hubris of the neoliberals and raised the spectre of an alternative. But the optimism of the left around the time of Seattle, whose various factions anticipated a speedy advance, and perhaps even a breakthrough into mass politics, has certainly subsided in the period since. The depth of the radicalisation we witnessed in the early 2000s actually went far beyond anything that we have seen since Lehman Brothers collapsed in 2008.

In Italy, there were huge protests outside the G8 summit in the summer of 2001, which while joined by a wealth of activists from abroad, primarily consisted in a vast mobilisation of the Italian radical movement. Two days of direct action saw tens of thousands participate and the young activist, Carlo Giuliani, murdered by the Italian police in a breathtaking bout of state violence. Attempts to split the civil disobedience wing of the movement from the Italian working class followed as it was denounced viciously in the media and by world leaders at the summit, but this failed abysmally as a huge protest of the Italian unions and social movements, numbering some 250,000 people, took place after the two days of clashes. It laid the basis for several years of significant mobilisation in Italy that was imbued with a powerful anticapitalistic and revolutionary fervour, of which the demonstration in Rome in February 2003 formed but only one cog with a wider process of growing upheaval. Yet the protests in Italy, and other countries where mobilisation approached this scale, continually ran up against the political question. In its leadership and overall ethos the social forum movement in Europe took its model of anticapitalism from Latin American, where social mobilisation was juxtaposed to the formation of left populist governments. But no such avenues opened up in Europe, largely due to hegemony that neoliberalised social democracy retained at the level of mass politics, and attempts to open up a "Latin American road", such as the Italian party Rifondazione Comunista's decision to enter the Prodi government, meant falling behind this project. Unprepared to take the movement in a more overtly political direction, for example towards new parties which could challenge the hegemony of neoliberalised social democracy in wider society, the social forums were relatively defenceless as world politics stabilised again in the mid-part of the last decade.

Summit sieges and social forums: recalling the anticapitalist movement

Looking back at this process of radicalisation it is difficult not to be struck by the crucial role played by ideology in stimulating and developing resistance. The original anticapitalist protests were ignited through a feeling of disillusionment with the realities of a global order in which politics no longer gave rise to any kind of clash of ideology and, so, this kind of contestation was pushed onto the streets. Even as the movement became larger, it was often ideological principles, which held the key to the mobilisation rather than raw, economic imperative to fightback that we have seen during the course of the financial crisis. Of course, this is not to say that neoliberal restructuring is unrelated to the economic structure, for, on the contrary, it actually reflects many of its exigencies, but opposing something such as privatisation requires a consciousness of its likely effects and why it will be harmful for the labour force and society rather than simply an immediate interest in stopping job or wage cuts.

Neither did all those millions who marched against the war do so on the basis of any immediate economic interest or incentive. They did so out of revulsion not only at the obviously dishonest justification for the conflict, the non-existent "weapons of mass destruction", but the whole concept of a "war without end" on enemies defined so broadly they included any state or movement perceived to challenge American interests. The same can equally be said of the upsurge of discontent in the West against the use of sweatshops and the third world debt, which expressed international solidarity and not a collective economic self-interest of western workers. In other words, these were all mobilisations that were fundamentally about the *type of society* we wanted to live in.

The relationship of this ideological discontent with the status quo and the economic, structural condition of globalisation in the early 2000s is in some respects curious.

This was a time when deflation in commodity prices and spiralling credit was making up for stagnating wages and some workers, such as teachers in Britain, actually realised significant increases in their incomes. Indeed, the globe-trotting activity of the anticapitalist activists of that time, jumping from summit to summit, forum to forum, was helped in no small part by the booming no frills aviation industry, something that would often cause consternation amongst many environmental activists in the movement. But as the excitement surrounding this single tactic inevitably dissipated then a broader political perspective was needed. Ultimately, the lack of this, and the fact that the economic stability of capitalism from 2004 to 2008 was simply not especially conducive to the popularising an anti-systemic critique, led the movement to decline.

In the end, the anticapitalist movement suffered from is a continual narrowing of its horizons as it drifted rightwards away from its original anticapitalist ethos, towards the more ambiguous "another world is possible" and concluding with the politics of *altermondialism* encapsulated by the social reform agenda for the EU. Perfectly collapsing the betwixt and between dilemma, it was no coincidence that this occurred with the entry of large sections of the organised labour movement in Europe and left populism in Latin America through the course of the social forums. The relative stability in the conjunctural structure of globalisation in the middle of the last decades simply created circumstances more favourable to this drift to the right. But it underlines the importance of a radical, anti-systemic critique that genuinely seeks to articulate, indeed which raises consciousness of, the need for a fundamental socialist transformation of our global society. But, while we should keep in mind this critique of the movement's trajectory, there are still numerous positive lessons to draw from the pattern of mobilisation we saw from Seattle onwards.

The left has been at its strongest when it has brought about a living unity between the new social movements and the working class; in Seattle, this was the Teamster-Turtle alliance (union members and environmentalists); in Britain, back in 2003, it was the anti-war movement, backed by almost every trade union in the country and with a strong, relatively united organisation, the Stop the War coalition, behind it. In Egypt, last year, the mass protests in Tahrir square set the scene for a resurgence of the workers' movement, with escalating strikes breaking out across the economy, putting the final nail in the coffin of the Mubarak regime. When this unity has not been struck we have suffered. In the resistance to austerity in Britain, the missing element is the development of a real, organic unity between the anti-cuts movement and the trade union members feeling the effects of cuts in the workplace. Not simply mass protests – these have been integral to the work of the left – but the development of solid links between the anti-cuts movement, which is, unlike the official tops of union structures in their majority, opposed to all cuts *and* grassroots trade unionists feeling their effect as workers and service users. The latter need to find their confidence and political strength in the radicalism of the social movement just as the movement should not treat the working class as one interest group amongst many, but, if conceived in suitably broad and encompassing terms, the key lever of progressive, fundamental social change.

The post-1999 social movements have shown that potentially millions can be thrown into a struggle and resistance to capitalism and for a fundamental social change. But for all the ideological impetus that drove many of these movements, they also, paradoxically, gave expression to the post-political logic that engulfed the world after 1989, because the social forums were consciously limited to the task of aggregating together diverse campaigns in a manner that retained their *social movement* as opposed to *political movement* character. It is not that the forums were not highly political – they were. These events bore witness to a veritable outpouring of political discussion on a vast array of themes. But they ultimately lacked a strategic perspective for social transformation; a strategy to move from protest to a real challenge for power. And it is the latter that would have necessitated a discussion around new political formations as part of a process of attempting to cohere together what Marxists have traditionally referred to as an 'international', i.e. a global political party that seeks to overcome national antagonisms and move towards the transcendence of capital.[122]

Due largely to its anti-party rules, it was in parallel to the social forum movement that new political formations on the left emerged that were seeking to contest neoliberalism in the electoral sphere. While this hardly chimed with the radical direct action of the anticapitalist movement at its most exciting, such initiatives were nonetheless necessary in order to reach out to the great majority of working class people whose primary, active interaction with politics is still limited, almost exclusively, to the electoral terrain. Most of the radical left recognised the opportunity for this, at least from the early 2000s onwards, as the rightist drift of social democracy opened up avenues for new alternative political parties. Whether it is Rifondazione Comunista (Italy), Die Linke (Germany), Left Bloc (Portugal), P-SOL (Brazil), Syriza (Greece), the NPA (France), Front de Gauche (France), and many others, the tendency to the emergence of new parties of the left has been a defining feature of left wing politics over the last decade. In some ways, these parties represented a return to the kind of broad working class and Marxist parties that were formed by the Second International prior to the First World War. At least, insofar as they did, in principle, bring together reformist and revolutionary currents in a tense cohabitation within a common political party. We say "in principle", because some parties, such as Rifondazione Comunista, were in their majority reformist parties with a small revolutionary minority, whereas the various projects of the British left, from the Socialist Alliance to Respect, tended to be dominated by the revolutionary left in terms of their composition, but cloaked themselves in reformist language and politics in the hope of significantly increasing their popular appeal. It is certainly likely that such parties will emerge time and again in the years ahead as expressions of the fact that large sections of the working class are likely to find their way to radical politics as a result of coming around parties that go beyond the existing left. These are important attempts to find a way to the masses and overcome the left's isolation.

While recognising the positive aspects of these projects we also have to remain conscious that attempts to suspend the strategic divergence between reform and revolution indefinitely are ultimately ill-fated. Rosa Luxemburg's original point is often posed purely in terms of the *different goal* – a socially moderated capitalism – that reformism offers in contrast to the socialist vision, but she also emphasised the different methods that revolutionary socialists utilise to fight for reforms. Because this involves immediate issues of how we choose to resist capitalism it can drive a sharp wedge between reformist and revolutionaries, one which threatens the unity of a unitary left party. Once again this returns to the "betwixt and between" problematic and attempts to build new formations over the last period have been plagued by the operative antagonisms reformist and revolutionary perspectives introduced into such formations. A line is easy to draw when it comes to those parties who have entered capitalist governments and propped up coalitions carrying through neoliberal reforms. From the very earliest stage of its development, Die Linke in Germany revealed its reformist orientation by its support for neoliberal reforms of social housing in Berlin and the track record of the PDS (a social democratic party whose origins lie in the old ruling party of the GDR) in municipal and state government in eastern German provinces. A similar process occurred in Italy, although it did so within a political terrain marked by substantial political radicalisation and mass protest, when twice Rifondazione Comunista entered the neoliberal government of Romano Prodi. On the second occasion this was foreshadowed by a turn away from street protest in 2004. With elections approaching RC leader Fausti Bertinotti led it back into Prodi's Olive Tree Coalition on the basis that the electoral defeat of Silvio Berlusconi was the overwhelming priority. The result was the bitter punishment of Rifondazione Comunista at the 2008 as they lost all their seats in parliament.

The challenge for the radical left is that because our project is largely based on utilising extra-parliamentary avenues into politics – from occupations, to general strikes, grassroots movements in the unions to fighting for workplace democracy – our "programme" requires a level of practical activity that goes far beyond the normal level of involvement most working class people are use to, which is usually limited to voting or signing a petition. The excitement of Italy during the high point of its radicalisation in the last decade lay in the level of activity and ideological ferment that emerged. The growth of local social forums around Genoa, 2001, extended this into local communities, and the packed out European Social Forum in Florence 2002 – whose fort *Belvedere* was transformed into a vast radical conference with tens of thousands of participants discussing anticapitalism – put Italy at the centre of a global movement at the time referred to as "the second superpower".[123] This offered glimmers, to us at least, of what a society would look like as its working classes were beginning to create a new society in the shell of the old. But conditions like these have been the exception rather than the norm in the years prior to the financial crisis; confined in particular to Latin America where the social movements were strongest, and partly to France and Italy (though even in Italy it was never reflected in *really substantial* electoral success, for example, at its high point in 2006 Rifondazione Comunista won 7.4 per cent of the vote). A temptation in this context is to fall behind fairly consolidated, reformist left parties, such as *DieLinke* in Germany as if "this is all that is possible" and certainly the all-pervasiveness of capitalist realism makes this an attractive option for even minimal alternatives somehow appear radical. But the problem is that in their search for credibility they either end up following the neoliberal road or presenting left reformist answers – with no prospect of winning office – that appear no more credible than an anticapitalist perspective in the eyes of wide layers of workers. Practice always "intervenes" into these perspectives because the reality of electoral office poses testing questions of where these parties stand. The Green Party in England and Wales, for instance, has never hidden the fact it has a largely electoralist orientation as a party. Notwithstanding the role individual Green Party members might play in building social struggle or the demonstrations its leaders will address, its ultimate priority has always been elections. But it is no coincidence therefore that when in municipal office, its councillors have voted through cuts rather than using their refusal to pass on cuts to build and develop extra-parliamentary resistance to the Tories.

For activists, the critical question is how these new formations and parties approach drawing into active social struggle and mobilisation the working classes; do they treat them as mere election fodder or do they have a perspective that is extra-parliamentary, active rather than passive? There are two particular examples of new formations in Europe that emphasised the "active" course. The New Anticapitalist Party (NPA) in France emerged through a fusion of the Trotskyist *Ligue Communiste Révolutionnaire* with new layers of activists from the social movements in 2009. A process of formation began after the 2007 presidential elections which saw LCR candidate Olivier Besancenot win over a million votes, a figure that surpassed the historically strong French communist party and was equivalent to the combined total of other left candidates. The NPA drew a clear line of demarcation with the French Socialist Party, refusing on point of principle to countenance entering government with it due to its record of neoliberal reforms and challenged many features of capitalist realism and the problems of the post-war left. It created a counter-hegemony around the figure of Oliver Besancenot whose militancy and youth helped popularise radical anticapitalism; it was an open, democratic and plural party, which provided a space that partially transcended the sect-form of post-war Trotskyism, helping to create a culture favourable to the renewal of Marxism and attractive to new layers of young people. A very similar project on a smaller scale was launched in the same year in Greece called Antarsya (the Alliance of the Anti-Capitalist Left), which sought to draw together groupings on the radical left and new layers of activists. These projects combine openness and pluralism with an openly revolutionary and anticapitalist perspective; the Marxist view that the act of emancipation of the working class will come through its own actions, its own struggles, rather than parliamentary reform. This makes these projects attractive examples for our argument; they represent attempts to transcend the "sect logic" of the left but ones that still retain a genuine anticapitalist perspective and so explicitly challenge capitalist realism.

The reformist temptation? The problems of articulating anticapitalism

Yet the experiences of the NPA and Antarsya are both somewhat negative. These parties have both been eclipsed by left reformist rivals, which are similar in their political composition to Rifondazione Comunista in Italy. The last French election saw Jean-Luc Melenchon, of the Left Front, a split from the French Socialist Party win nearly 11 per cent of the vote while support for the NPA collapsed to just over 1 per cent – down nearly 7 per cent on 2007.[124] In Greece, Syriza (the Coalition of the Radical Left) nearly won the second general election in 2012 as the depth of the nation's social crisis forced a dramatic political polarisation. This compared to just over 1 per cent support Antarsya had won. The second election after no government could be formed led to an either larger gap between the results of Syriza and Antarsya. The two experiences are distinct, not least because Antarsya never achieved the size or electoral success of the NPA or its precursor the LCR, is operating in a radically different environment of abject social breakdown (Greece is the only European country in the post-war period to have experienced a five year long recession), and the decline of the NPA has subjective as well as objective factors. But these experiences together illustrate the enduring appeal of left reformism, which does not make the demands of militant mobilisation on an electorate, but still appears to offer radical change. These hopes may well be illusory, but this criticism of reformism from the left will only carry "punch" if extra-parliamentary resistance is seen to offer a living alternative to it that can actualise real hope in an entirely different society. Indeed, there is a reason, ultimately, that Greece has now polarised in the way that it has, because of the sheer desperation that the economic crisis has forced upon whole swathes of society that makes radical alternatives attractive. It is also not coincidental that there have been no revolutions of an insurrectionary character in Western Europe since 1848. The combination of liberal democracy, capitalist development, and the ideology and practice of social mobility politics, was able to create class alliances that rendered these states relatively stable in contrast to the rest of the world.

The question, of course, is whether the new period opened in 2008 actually creates a crisis on a sufficient depth that it starts to fracture the kinds of class alliances that capitalist elites in the West successfully fostered and on which liberal democracy has long depended. In this context, left reformism is attractive precisely because it *offers the path of least resistance,* i.e. it promises not an equal society but a set of social reforms that might make a situation such as the people have faced in Greece bearable. The challenge for the left will be learning how to relate to this in a manner that both understands the real reasons these parties have proven to be attractive, but also offers a fundamental alternative to the never ending conflicts and struggles fostered by capitalism: i.e. is able to convince new layers of people that genuinely working class forms of direct democracy that reach into the workplace and undertake collective economic planning in the interests of the people offers a viable alternative to the market. Keeping in mind the extra-parliamentary dimensions – be they workplace or social movement based – to our political strategy is crucial in this regard. In the debate that has erupted in the New Anticapitalist Party over how it should account from bursting forward to organise 10,000 members only to then fall backwards to around 3 to 4,000 many activists have identified how an obsession with elections was often combined with the idea that left reformism in a traditional sense had run its course.[125] Many of the public statements of Olivier Besancenot envisaged a situation in which "social liberalism", i.e. neoliberalised social democracy, would now compete with "anticapitalism" and thus leave traditional forms of reformist politics in the pages of history.[126] These understated the scale of the task at hand but they also fed into an excessive focus on trying to seize the electoral space over and above developing extra-parliamentary forms of mobilisation. It did not help that crossing the 5 per cent barrier in elections also meant gaining access to considerable amounts of money from the state – something that highlights how harmful money in general (however necessary), and the state's money in particular, can be.

Activists who were involved in the NPA often cite the way in which it was organised as a factor in its decline. To its credit the NPA embraced plurality, but it did so in a form that internalised aspects of sect politics – *a la* the highly homogenous propaganda current –into its party life. To have a stake and political influence within the NPA it is necessary to a member of one of other of its numerous factional platforms. Attendance at its congresses could therefore be a peculiar experience, because the outcome was often known in advanced, based on the relative numbers mobilised by its various tendencies. The result was debates could become polarised, but there was also little attempt to arrive and arrive at some kind of common methodological principles – as if no such common position were possible and that its internal divisions were somehow inevitable.

A similar problem – in the sense that it illustrates some of the dangers involved in trying to overcome the top-down and bureaucratic logic of traditional left wing organisation – existed when it came to the extent of the autonomy granted to local branches and regions. Undoubtedly this was a good thing, it made the NPA a democratic and participatory organisation, but activists ended up complaining that there was little in the way of nationally-focused political campaigning. In periods of upsurge in the French class struggle, such as the pensions' dispute in 2010, the NPA had nothing like the profile or impact it should have done, had it not formed structures that were consciously co-ordinating its attempts to develop the movement from below. It is not necessarily a question of striking a "balance" between leadership and democracy, but recognising that for democracy to be real it has to involve the formation of authoritative national bodies mandated to carry out the will of the collective organisation. The autonomy of base organisations and, indeed, of individuals, then needs to be mediated so that a balance is struck between granting a healthy amount of freedom and recognising "majoritarianism" in the daily practice of the political organisation. If there is a lesson here it is that overcoming bureaucratic and top down models of party organisation and trying to pioneer a new way of doing things is a noble endeavour but nonetheless also carries with it dangers too.

Although formed in the same year, the Greek alliance Antarsya was always radically different in logic to the NPA. It grouped together small radical communist groupings and gave them a common platform with which they could have an electoral profile and reach while also providing avenues for an increased profile in the protest and strike movements. But one of the positive features of the NPA was always that in forming it the LCR took the decision to dissolve their existing organisation and establish a new grouping with a strong, organic connection to new layers of activists. As Daniel Bensaïd pointed out,[127] this actually gave the project real credibility and illustrated their seriousness to activists from the social movements with whom they had worked alongside across the last decade. Antarsya, in contrast, was always an alliance of independent organisations. But in 2012 it would share with the NPA the experience of being outflanked by a grouping to its right. Syriza, as its name *Coalition* of the Radical Left suggests, drew together broad layers from eurocommunists that dominated its leadership, to Maoists, Trotskyists, and libertarian, non-aligned activists. Given the tensions such a coalition would involve, it is perhaps unsurprising that it suffered a split in 2010 as the right-wing section of the parliamentary broke away to form Democratic Left, which left Syriza free to take a much more assertively anti-austerity stance and clearly associated itself with the rising tide of extraparliamentary resistance. As the crisis deepened over the next two years, it was able to storm to electoral prominence in 2012 after the decision of the conservative New Democracy to call early elections – hoping it would be the principle beneficiary of the collapse of the Pasok vote – badly backfired, it suddenly found itself on the cusp of power as new elections were called. A party that had won less than 5 per cent of the vote in 2009 won 26.89% of the vote in the second election of this year, coming a close second, within three percentage points of New Democracy.

Both the NPA and Antarsya took a conscious decision to try to organise a new political formation on positively anticapitalist lines. Undoubtedly this is something with enormous merit – especially when compared to the stale bureaucratism of parties like *Die Linke* in Germany. But both of them declined the invitation to enter a broader electoral coalition. In the case of the NPA this was perhaps more understandable, because, due to the machinations of the French political system, the Communist Party, a key component of the Left Front, was structurally dependent on alliances with the Socialist Party at municipal level (agreements not to stand against one another) and a successful candidature for Jean-Luc Melenchon was likely to result in entering a future Socialist Party dominated government. In an era of austerity this will reproduce the Prodi and Rifondazione Comunista scenario in Italy and carry with it electoral and political implications for those who supported it. Clearly understanding the concrete situation and the balance of forces is crucial in this regard. In Greece, it was similarly understandable that Antarsya was formed in opposition to the social reformism of Syriza's leadership that ultimately stood for a kind of austerity-lite politics. But several concrete factors speak in favour of Antarsya joining the coalition. The exit from Syriza of its right-wing parliamentary faction in 2010 was followed by its dramatic electoral success in the spring of 2012. This is coupled with the fact it is a heterogeneous coalition including Trotskyists and Maoists, i.e., very far from a normal reformist party, and actually invited Antarsya to join its coalition at the June 2012 election. All of which makes the decision to stay outside is perplexing. If millions of workers are coming behind such an initiative that is promoting an end to austerity, surely the radical left must try and influence its development? Some of the arguments used in relation to the debate also reveal worrying tendencies. In his piece, back in 2010, Stathis Kouvelakis actually identified Antarsya as a grouping that had tried to overcome the distinction between "propagandist attitudes and syndicalist agitation" by developing a concrete, revolutionary perspective for Greece to move out of the crisis: a default on its debts, a sweeping wave of nationalisation without compensation and developing real forms of workers' power from below.[128] But, while these points have appeared in their statements, they have also tended to identify themselves as the grouping calling for an "uprising" and even said that strikes and the streets, not elections, is where matters will ultimately decided.[129] Calling for uprisings may help them appeal to the most radical sections, but workers will want answers to their social blight. Few are likely to respond to the call for yet more uprisings – there have been numerous such mobilisations in Greece – but will want to know how Antarsya's politics will change their life. It is quite wrong, as some international supporters of Antarsya have argued, that strikes and the streets and not elections is where the struggle will be decided; for it is impossible to separate the two. Upon their electoral breakthrough in May 2012, Syriza called for local assemblies and the base of the party expanded outwards into vast outdoor local meetings; so the impact of the election was to inspire mobilisation that, if it was consciously extended could, in principle, lay the basis for a profound transformation towards direct democracy. To abstain from the struggle over Syriza's future direction, should, that is, it successfully take power, and instead criticise from the sidelines, revealed highly "propagandistic attitudes".

That this debate is happening, however, is encouraging, because in Greece there has been "a return of strategy" and, depending on the outcome of the elections, this may be extended across Europe as the neoliberal assumptions of capitalist realism are ruptured. There is a potential for a workers' government which bases its rule not on the institutions of the bourgeois state, even though it will likely come into being through the mainstream election process, but seeks to establish forms of direct democracy based on the working class.[130] This perspective is arguably what the radical left should be pushing for within Syriza and is a policy that will inevitably open up antagonisms within the coalition over the true meaning of an anti-austerity politics. In the *mêlée* of cultural and political antagonisms distilled out of the economic crisis finding a path betwixt and between abstention from living struggle and accommodation to the still reformist consciousness of the masses, one that can result in the formation of "workers' governments", is perhaps the central question facing the radical left.

In few countries, however, is the revolutionary left have anything like the "problems " that have been encountered in France and Greece; in both situations new, radical political formations were forged that however momentarily in the case of France nonetheless had a real and genuine impact on the political consciousness of wider society. The creation of new forms of political organisation which draw upon the spirit of the social movements, rekindle grassroots trade union organisation, and embolden participation of wider sections of society in social mobilisations is an orientation on which the success of the left ultimately depends.

Drawing conclusions

If we think of capitalism as fluid, with constantly shifting plates of the social and political delicately interspersed with the raw accumulation demands of its economy, then we see a system in constant movement and perpetual transformation. The scope and speed of these changes has increased markedly since the collapse of Lehman Brothers as the cogs of the machine are increasingly greased with the livelihoods of working people and the poor.

The interconnected and transformative nature of capitalism also provides the key to how it can be disrupted and ultimately overturned. Particularly in conditions of global economic crisis – when the world economy has undergone several decades of increasing integration – we live in world in which disruption to the movements of capital at one point in the system can have a powerful impact on the system as a whole. By which we mean not only the rhythms of economic crisis, but also the ways in which ideological, social, and cultural forms of resistance in one place, at one moment of time, can spread outwards across the system.

And the prospects for an end to capitalism realism are good. In *Why It's Kicking Off Everywhere*, Mason has argued, perhaps prematurely, that "the age of capitalist realism has ended" with the Egyptian revolution. We would not go that far - in as much as the Arab spring is similar to the 1848 revolutions in Europe they happen within the parameters of a democratic and liberal politics and so do not involve a direct challenge to capitalism. However, the wider crisis that has engulfed the world points to two key factors in the unravelling of capitalist ideological hegemony. We mentioned before that the strength of neoliberalism after 1991 was that it made democracy and modernity synonymous with the market. Today, that connection is badly frayed. In the wake of corruption scandals across the media, banking and political establishments, then, who, now, can honestly say that the markets create democracy? When faced with a decade lost to austerity and a young generation with a worse standard of living than their parents and grandparents, who can honestly claim with a straight face that capitalism will guarantee modernity and progress? In the face of rising police powers and authoritarianism, rampant corruption across major institutions and declining living standards, capitalism *as democracy* appears less "realistic".

Which is why, we might add, that capitalist elites fight so ferociously. The intensity of contemporary attacks on labour by capital has a character similar to what Antonio Gramsci referred to as the "war of manoeuvre".[131] For Gramsci, this was the insurrectionary moment in revolutionary politics; the once and for all push for fundamental social change that if it were attempted permanently would only result in defeat and the marginalisation of the left, but if it were avoided at all costs could never deliver victory. Yet capital has an advantage of being at the ruling apex of a class structure, which is able through subterranean means to cultivate a culture of social mobility to disguise this on-going increase in social inequality and injustice, the war of manoeuvre is, thus, an attractive, indeed essential means to continually re-create conditions favourable to its self-expansion.

How to respond to this is one of the basic problems of left wing politics; we need to find a means through which to build social strength and power overtime – the "war of position" – and simultaneously challenge through our own "offensive" actions against the seemingly perpetual insurrection against working class living standards. In the communist movement of the 1920s and later amongst the Trotskyists of the 1930s, the tactical-strategic answer was conceived along the lines of "transitional demands".[132] These were policies that when taken up by large sections of the working class inevitably brought them into conflict with capital, for they challenged its monopoly over the running of the "economic sphere", with demands for workers' control in industry and the abolition of business secrecy. In the absence of the labour movement establishing a new type of state that could render these gains permanent by generalising democratic control of the economy across society, then such demands were temporally circumscribed because ruling capitalist elites would not tolerate this interference over their informal monopoly over all aspects of economic life for any length of time. But they would open up an antagonism between labour and capital through which the true nature of the system might be exposed, laying the way open for social revolutionary change.

The point of this perspective was not necessarily to engage in dry "programme writing", for which the Trotskyist movement has been not unjustly criticised in the past, but to try and advocate social struggles that empower labour over capital. But the problem came with the decline of the left and the bureaucratisation of the labour movement, because by virtue of this rightward shift these proposals tended to be relegated to the programme of the sect rather than crystallized in the living struggles of the workers' movement against capital. In terms of the demands that the left raised in struggle, they tend to be defensive and rarely offensive, and this is reflective of the simple fact that the workers' movement lacks in most countries the strength of social organisation that could make these demands credible. The conclusion to draw is that reorganising the workers' movement from below is surely an essential precondition for undertaking these kinds of incursions on the power of capital.

The argument presented here has moved between a number of elements, so to make explicit our conclusions then we can summarise in a few points the crux of our message:

- **The crisis of the left *is still* a crisis of the sect.** Sometimes referred to as the idea of a "fighting propaganda group", the left group with a narrowly conceived strategy and tradition that acts as a "monopolist in the sphere of politics", is a model that fundamentally disrupts the development of organic unity on the left.

- **The drive to new political formations,** although it is rarely understood in these terms, is a response to a reality that a sect-ridden left is a left that will inevitable fail. These new formations are a reality of left politics in the early 21st century, they express an attempt to build organisations that go beyond the fragments and thus have a genuine credibility. Where these formations have been at their best, they have gone beyond an electoral alliance of competing parts and tried to establish the conditions for an embracing unity that genuinely transcends the "sect form".

- **Strategy beyond the sects – an evolving process.** Developing a strategy to move beyond capitalism will have to draw on a vast array of experiences and ideas. Despite Marxists often holding religiously to the idea that programme as a guide to action with the collapse of the socialist movement into a sect existence, the formulation of programme became bound up with the development of ossified traditions. If we are to move beyond this, we have to see the formulation of strategy as an evolving process. Radical manifestos should be conceived not as timeless abstractions unmediated by the rhythms of social change, but as guides continually tested, reappraised and rearticulated as lessons are drawn from victories and defeats. In this way, we can move beyond the tendency to combine syndicalist agitation with a propagandistic attitude, by rejecting the all-or-nothing approach to programme (either the "full revolutionary programme" or limited demands) and try and develop an elastic, flexible, but still principled, approach to articulating anti-systemic politics.

- **A pluralistic Marxism is needed.** The idea of Marxism as a science that seeks to appropriate knowledge about the world that can be objectively proven, has often, particularly when it becomes incorporated into a narrowly conceived "tradition", led to monopolistic conclusions about "right and wrong" approaches. But if we conceive of Marxism as a collective process involving many practitioners then it is possible to see different viewpoints as contributing to the common evolution of a genuinely scientific body of thought. While this process is always contested, and always involves competing claims to truth and falsity that can indeed be objectively proven one way or the other, we need to also recognise the role that a plurality of diverse and different viewpoints must play in avoiding the trap of an ossified Marxism.

- **Practice-informed strategic thinking is required.** By creating new forums for strategic discussion – in which different visions can co-exist in a certain tension – but also allow for their mediation into the rhythms of political action, then we can move towards a more flexible, more living conception of revolutionary programme. A strategy however well codified is of little use to the working class unless it can find its mediation into practice, and new layers of activists are coming together – be they in the labour movement of Occupy – that want to develop an anti-authoritarian left wing politics. An effective strategy is something that will be formulated in alliance with these layers, and undertaking this process of renewal has the positive consequence that it forces the left to put forward its politics in concrete terms.

- **Reclaim democracy as a left wing idea.** If there is a lesson of 2011 it is that the left will fail to answer the challenges of our century unless it can show that democracy is a thoroughly left wing idea. On the one hand, this must mean promoting the radical extension of democracy into the workplace and civic community and so counter-pose direct, active, living democratic structure to the dry and alienating bureaucratism of its liberal so-called "representative" incarnation. On the other hand, the left needs to cease seeing the struggle for individual freedoms and the right of self-expression as somehow alien to its collectivist ideals, and instead recognise that a living and dynamic collective can only come into being if it is built in a constant process of reciprocal dialogue with the struggle for free individuality.

- **A credible extra-parliamentary politics.** If we are to overcome our own propagandistic tendencies we have to be able to show that extra-parliamentary political struggle can offer credible solutions to working class people. Avoiding advancing the crude syndicalism that says elections don't matter and strikes do is crucial. Who governs and in whose interest remains a critical question for working people in the face of a political offensive of austerity on our hard won collective gains. But we need to do this in full knowledge of the "betwixt and between" balancing act of not holding out a utopia that the structures of representative democracy and electoralism can somehow resolve the crisis. We need a radical extension of democracy into our communities and economic life. This is the difference between "reformist" and revolutionary conceptions of politics that imposes itself with a great deal of immediacy in the new conditions of austerity.

- **Build grassroots movements "from below".** It is a truism for those who still believe in the "working class subject" that change will come through "the masses" and their organisations. But we also have to square up to the fact that many working class institutions have undergone a century of bureaucratisation and incorporation into the strictures of capital. This does not necessarily mean trying to build

"new unions", but it does mean building parallel organisations based on the grassroots, unencumbered by bureaucracy, and prepared to fight with the official leaders
wherever possible, but also without them wherever
necessary. That builds, in short, an independent pole based
on social struggle from below rather than relying on the
bureaucratised hierarchies. This will also allow the unions
to free themselves from the confines of narrow economic
terms and open outwards to the array of urban and rural
class struggles – which arise out of the multiple means
capital exploits subaltern layers – that mark our age.

- **The labour struggle *is always* a social struggle.** Occupy's
desire to reclaim a space of resistance to capital was not
something external to a working class politics, but a
feature of how class politics will be reconceived in more
social terms in our age given the long retreat of labour and
workplace organisation. No labour struggle is likely to be
successful without utilising social movement activism;
building solidarity with wider layers of the community
and drawing them in behind the movement in a wave of
popular mobilisation. Indeed, all mass workers'
movements have always had to take on this dimension –
from the Soviets of Working*Men* and Soldiers' Deputies of
1917 that drew behind them women, peasants and
students, to the British *Miners'* Strike of 1984 that
mobilised entire pit communities to defend a way of life –
the actual rhythms of class struggle have always broken
free from a narrowly economic vocabulary. This also alerts
us to the form the social revolutions of the future will take;
that they will desire not only workplace power, but also a
civic democracy – extending, for instance, to a fight for a
democratic control over banking institutions – and seeking
to base this on the direct democracy of working class
communities.[133]

We believe these points, taken together, can help the left to move beyond isolation and find a way through the old dilemma that Rosa Luxemburg famously outlined. In navigating the "betwixt and between" problematic, flexibility and fluidity in organisation, searching out new avenues for unity, will be essential. If there is a lesson in the triumph of neoliberalism it is that flexibility and pragmatism in how you take forward a conflict is crucial to helping foster the sense that "you are the pragmatists" and those who challenge you are the doctrinaire immobilizers who are clinging to privileges won in a bygone past. Here, then, the left needs to seize hold of a terrain of radical "common sense", to break free from the idea that a radical alternative to the market is somehow utopian, to expose how social extremism emerges ineluctably from market-worship, and present a forward-looking vision.

The appeal to common sense is crucial to breakdown doctrinaire assumptions on the radical left and try to overcome divisions between the "old and new". It also emphasises the need to regroup the left in new political formations that provide a space for strategic thinking, that allow different strategies to co-exist in a certain tension, while also creating the conditions for unity and action. The spirit of "one no, many yeses" needs to be instilled in these formations. Not, though, as an excuse to avoid reflective, strategic discussion but as a starting point through which we can move towards a greater degree of genuine unity.

References

1   Bigelow, M L. 2010, *TGC 70. Prof. Lester Thurow, "The Future of Capitalism."* http://vimeo.com/17338846 (Accessed 26 July 2012).

2   Hope, K., 2012, 'OECD predicts decades of austerity lie ahead for UK' 13 April 2012

3   Rove, K., cited in Mason, P., 2012, *Why it's kicking off everywhere*; the new global revolutions, Verso: London, p. 31 – 32

4   Braudel, F., 1960, "History and the Social Sciences: The Long Duration." *American Behavioral Scientist* 3 (6) (February 1): 3 –13. p. 3 – 4

5   Ibid

6   Trotsky, L., 1923, "The curve of capitalist development" http://www.marxists.org/archive/trotsky/1923/04/capdevel. htm (Accessed 30 June 2012).

7   Harvey, D., 2010, *The Enigma of Capital,* Oxford University Press, Oxford. p. 10 – 11.

8   Harvey, D., 2011, "The Party of Wall Street Meets its Nemesis" www.versobooks.com/blogs/777   (Accessed 26 June 2012).

9   PolitiFact.Com 2009 'During the Reagan era, "the richest Americans had their top income tax rate cut in half."' http://bit.ly/FWmg3 (Accessed 30 July 2012). On productivity see Politifact.com 2009 'Michael Moore claims in "Capitalism" that during Reagan years, productivity went up while wages remained frozen' http://bit.ly/W9Q Ou (Accessed 30 July 2012).

10   Liberto J., 2012, "CEO pay is 380 times average worker's - AFL-CIO" at Moneycnn.com (Accessed 30 July 2012).

11   Gramsci, A., 1971, *Gramsci: Selections from the Prison Notebooks* International Publisher: New York, p276

12   Hatherley, O., "Something has snapped, and it has

been a long time coming" www.versobooks.com/blogs/660 (Accessed 14 May 2012).

13   Orwell, G., 2004, *1984* 1st World Publishing: Fairfield, IA, p334

14   Fisher, M., 2011. "The Privatisation of Stress" newleft-project.org (Accessed 14 May 2012).

15   Anderson, P., 2000, "Renewals" New Left Review, 1 January-February, p17

16   Cox, C., Whalen, M., and Badiou, A., 2001 "On Evil: An Interview with Alain Badiou" www.cabinetmagazine .org/issues/5/alainbadiou.php (Accessed 1 June 2012).

17   Friedman, M. and Friedman, R D., 2002, *Capitalism and Freedom* University of Chicago Press: Chicago

18   Bensaïd, D., 2011, *La Politique comme art stratégique* (Politics as a Strategic Art). Editions Syllepse: Paris, p28.

19   Marx, Karl. 1978, *18th Brumaire of Louis Bonaparte,* Foreign Languages Press: Beijing, p9.

20   Ibid

21   Anon, "Video: Battle of the Iron Ladies as miners' wives picket Maggie movie" Yorkshire Post website (Accessed: 14 May 2012).

22   Marx, K., 1987 *Marx and Engels Collected Works volume 28* Lawrence and Wishart: London, p. 95

23   Marcuse, H., 2002, *One-Dimensional Man: Studies in the Ideology of Advanced Industrial Society,* Routledge,

24   Marx, K., 1970, Capital Volume 1, Lawrence and Wishhart: London p. 751. In this case the allegory is almost literal, there are no more need of midwives, there is no future left to give birth to.

25   Jameson, Frederick. 2003, "Future City", New Left Review 21, May-June 2003

26   The Star Trek canon actually offers two answers; neither of which affirms the idea that "the revolution happened". Although Star Trek has been heavily criticised by the

American political right for its "communism", the canon actually sidesteps whether social revolution is needed to achieve a classless society. Like much science fiction, its appeal partly lies in the fact that it keeps alive an optimistic sense of utopia, a system of exciting universal ideals, outside of the drudgery and sameness of everyday life. In the Star Trek universe a devastating Third World War, with some 600 million deaths, brings civilisation to the brink of destruction before the development of 'warp capability' makes possible inter-galactic space travel. In the Star Trek film, First Contact, this leads the Vulcans to arrive on earth and help humanity overcome its domestic troubles. The closest the canon comes to offering a more class-based explanation of the transformation towards a classless society, is in Star Trek Deep Space Nine; Past Tense. The crew also fall back in time, to prior to the Third World War in the early 21st century, a time in which unemployment has become so endemic in the United States that open-air prisons called 'enclosures' have been established for the jobless. Despite being broadcast in the 1990s, this plotline has an unusual plausibility for the Star Trek canon given the return of large-scale homelessness and unemployment in the United States. It is actually an armed uprising in the enclosures that forces a shift in public opinion towards a new "New Deal" based on redistribution and social justice. Yet, it is not clear how this would prove ultimately to be a false dawn, as a Third World War broke out. Nonetheless, this second plotline does challenge the traditional conception that sees Star Trek's notion of progress as technologically deterministic, insofar as improvements in productive techniques create conditions for a classless society rather than it being an outcome of political design. In contrast, waiting for first contact with aliens to realise universal peace on earth is unlikely to be included in a sane political perspective. And, indeed, it is the ultimately farfetched nature of these pop culture portrayals of communism that underline the power of capitalist realism.

27 Fisher, Mark. *Capitalist Realism: is there no alternative?* Zero: London, p.4

28 Fukuyama, Francis. 1993, *The End of History and the Last Man.* Penguin: London, and New York

29 Hegel saw the culmination of history in the Prussian state of his day, which perfectly combined new forms of civil society with a traditional monarchy.

30 An exception – if they are considered part of the 'radical left' broadly defined – is the impact it had on the official parties of the communist movement, the Stalinists, who split and fragmented in the face of the collapse of the "mother party" in the Soviet Union, combining a combination of political despair with an almost total de facto acceptance of the triumph of liberalism. These ideological moves were foreshadowed by the rise of Eurocommunism in the 1970s, identified in Britain with the magazine *Marxism Today*.

31 Al Jazeera. "Zizek interviewed by Al Jazeera on world protests and Occupy Wall Street" http://www.rhizomia .net/2011/10/zizek-interviewed-by-al-jazeera-on.html (Accessed 10 May 2012).

32 Thanks to Ishan Cader for emphasising to us the importance of these cultural transformations for a rounded under-standing of the rise of neoliberalism and the defeat of the left.

33 Goethe, J W., 1999, *Faust part one*, Wordsworth: Ware, Herts p. 42

34 Sparrow, A. and Womack, S., 2002, "Union fury after Blair blames 'the wreckers'" The Telegraph, 04 February

35 Fisher, Mark. *Capitalist Realism*. Zero: London p.27-28

36 Mason, P., 2011, *Why It's Kicking Off Everywhere* Verso: London, p. 39.

37   Ibid, p. 45

38   Douzinas, C. and Žižek S., 2010, *The Idea of Communism*, Verso: London

39   Giddens, A., 1998, T*he Third Way: the renewal of social democracy.* Cambridge University Press: Cambridge, p. 43-44

40   This is a reference to a keynote speech by Tony Benn at the 1980 Labour Party Conference

41   Leys, C. 1996 "The British Labour Party's Transition From Socialism to Capitalism", *Socialist Register*(volume 32), p.8

42   Ibid p. 18

43   Arthur Scargill did attempt to set up the Socialist Labour Party, but the discussion of the sorry history of this neo-Stalinist project is far outside the scope of our concerns here.

44   Taylor, L., 2006, "Culture's revenge: Laurie Taylor inter-views Stuart Hall" http://newhumanist.org.uk/960/cultures-revenge-laurie-taylor-interviews-stuart-hall (Accessed 1 May 2012).

45   Morris, D., 1997, *Behind the Oval Office: winning the presi-dency in the nineties* Random House: New York, p.79

46   Hutton, W., 2011, "When we sold off the railways, we created today's shambles" Guardian, 22 May

47   Beckett, F., 2007, "Schools for scoundrels" http://newhu-manist.org.uk/1477/schools-for-scoundrels (Accessed 12 February 2012).

48   The Smith Institute published a briefing paper Hunter, P., 2011, "Winning back the 5 million; understanding the fragmentation of Labour's vote" available for download at www.smith-institute.org.uk (Accessed May 21 2012).

49   The story was broken by Liberal Conspiracy. Paskini, D., 2011, "Blue Labour founder: "Labour should involve EDL supporters"" http://liberalconspiracy.org/2011/04/21/blue-labour-founder-labour-should-involve-edl-supporters/

(Accessed 7 July 2012).

50   The Bell Pottinger group suffered an exposé by the Independent in December 2011, for boasting of high-level access to the coalition government and using their self described"dark arts" expertise to whitewash human rights abuses in Uzbekistan. They also advise the governments in Belarus and Bahrain and were previously hired by the Pinochet foundation named after the ex-Chilean dictator responsible for thousands of deaths.

51   Lansman, J., 2011, "Welcome to the Blairite Party-within-a-party" at www.leftfutures.org (Accessed 16 June 2012).

52   Eaton, G., 2011, "Labour's growing dependence on the unions" available at www.newstatesman.com (Accessed 26 June 2012).

53   Hicks, J.,2012, "Union leader slams Ed Miliband but who put him there in the first place?" www.jerryhicks4gs .com (Accessed 1 June 2012).

54   Choonara, E., 2011, "Is there a precariat?", Socialist Review, October 2011.

55   Standing, G., 2011, *The Precariat; The New Dangerous Class*, Bloomsbury Academic: London

56   For a stronger classical Marxist critique of the concept of the "precariat" see Seymour, Richard. 2012. "We Are All Precarious - On the Concept of the 'Precariat' and its Misuses" at newleftproject.org (Accessed 30 July 2012).

57   Ibid, p. 36 – 37.

58   Ibid, p. 41.

59   Trade Union Congress Commission on Vulnerable Work, 2007, *Hard Work, Hidden Lives*. p. 16.

60   Ibid

61   Ibid

62   Ibid, p. 10

63   Ibid

64   Grice, Andrew. 2011. "Cameron's war on employment

rights" www.independent.co.uk/news/uk/politics/cameron s-war-on-employment-rights-6266355.html (Accessed 14 July 2012).

65 Office for National Statistics, 2010. *Social Trends 40*, p. 53

66 Chapman, J., 2008, "60% of long-term benefits claimants 'could go back to work', admits minister" 07 August

67 BBC News. 2011 "Mental illness 'top reason to claim incapacity benefit'" www.bbc.co.uk/news/health-13309755 (Accessed 14 July 2012).

68 Colins, Chik., Dickson, Janice., Collins, Mary. 2009. *To Banker from Banksies; Incapacity Benefit: Myth and Realities*, p. 7

69 Stewart, Heather. 2012. "UK unemployment rises to 2.68m", 18 January

70 Ibid

71 Office for National Statistics. 2010. *Social Trends 40*, p. 53

72 Fisher, Mark. 2011. "The Privatisation of Stress" at newleft-project.org (Accessed 14 May 2012).

73 Anonymous, 2010. "How union membership has grown - and shrunk", Guardian, 30 April

74 Ibid

75 Ross, George. and Martin, Andrew. 1999 *The brave new world of European labor: European trade unions at the millennium*Berghahn Books: Oxford, p42

76 Roper, Carl. "Trade Union Membership 2010" strongerunions.org/2011/05/03/trade-union-member ship-2010/ (Accessed 13 May 2012).

77 Ibid

78 Roper, Carl. "Trade Union Membership – Steady As We Go" strongerunions.org/2010/05/18/trade-union-member ship-steady-as-we-go/ (Accessed 13 May 2012).

79 Fisher, Mark. *Capitalist Realism*. op cit, p.21

80 For the stats see: Roper, Carl. "Trade Union Membership 2010" strongerunions.org/2011/05/03/trade-union-member

ship-2010/ (Accessed 13 May 2012).

81 Speech at the Wembley Special Conference, 5 April 1982. Cited in Lang, John. and Dodkins, Graham. 2011. Bad News the Wapping Dispute. Spokesman Books: Nottingham

82 IRIS News, October 1982.

83 Cited in Sewell, Rob. 2003 "In the Cause of Labour" www.marxist.com/hbtu/chapter_23.html (Accessed 12 May 2012).

84 Cited in Bevin, Aneurin 1952 *In Place of Fear* EP Publishing: Michigan, p. 20 – 21

85 Ibid

86 Robins, J., 2005, "Card-carrying members will know that their unions have moved with the times, in one respect at least - their enthusiastic embrace of consumerism." "Why we're losing interest in union credit cards" 09 October

87 Bryson, A. and Forth, J., 2010. *Trade union membership and influence, 1999-2009*, NIESR Discussion Paper No. 362, p.2

88 Luxemburg, Rosa. 1908. *Reform or Revolution* "Chapter VII: Co-operatives, Unions, Democracy" (Accessed 30 July 2012).

89 Smith, Martin. 2011. "Britain's trade unions: the shape of things to come". International Socialism Journal issue 131.

90 Achur, J., 2010, Trade Union membership 2010, Department for Business Innovation and Skills

91 Heery, E., Simms, M., Delbridge, R., Salmon, J. and Simpson, D. 2000. "The TUCs Organising Academy: An Assessment." Industrial Relations Journal. 31:5, p. 99

92 TUC, 1994. *Campaigning for Change: A new era for the TUC* London: TUC, p.3

93 Smith, Martin. "Britain's trade unions: the shape of things to come" International Socialism Journal issue 131

94 Taken from Transcript of Andrew Marr show at http://bbc.in/NgRPMs

95 Ibid

96   Unite Press Release, 2010, "Unite calls for an alternative economic strategy to save jobs and boost demand" available at www.unitetheunion.org (Accessed 5 May 2012).

97   Anderson, K., 2011., "Time Person of the Year: the Protestor" 14 December 2011

98   PolitiFact.com 2009, "The richest 1 percent have more financial wealth than the bottom 95 percent combined." http://bit.ly/Ox0rS, (Accessed 14 May 2012).

99   Politifact. 2011. "Just 400 Americans — 400 — have more wealth than half of all Americans combined." http://bit.ly/fdXRU9 (Accessed 14 May 2012).

100 Elliott, J., 2011, "The origins of Occupy Wall Street explained" salon.com (Accessed 20 May 2012).

101 Ibid

102 Pham, B., 2011. "Occupy and the Tasks of Socialists" http://links.org.au/node/2657 (Accessed 14 July 2012).

103 el-Hamalawy, H., 2011 "Egypt's revolution has been 10 years in the making"02 March 2011

104 El-Mahdi, R. and Marfleet, P., 2009, *Egypt the Moment of Change.* Zed Books: London and New York

104 See debate amongst Jon Moses, Owen Jones, Maeve Mckeown and Luke Cooper on Open-Democracy: Moses, Jon. 2011 "In defence of black bloc", Jones, O., "The Black Bloc – a dead end (response to Jonathan Moses)"; Cooper, L., 2011, "Black Bloc: aesthetics won't beat the cuts" and Mckeown, M., 2011. "Black Bloc: A Self-Defeating Tactic?" http://studenttheory.wordpress.com/2011/04/04/black-bloc-a-self-defeating-tactic/ (Accessed 14 May 2012).

105 Marx, K., 1994, "Theses on Feuerbach" in *Marx's selected writings*, p. 98-101

106 This was a startling point made by Representative Thadeus McCotter. "McCotter Compares Bailout To Bolshevik Revolution In Russia" http://www.cbsnews.com/2100-501743_162-4485790.html (Accessed April 28 2012).

107 Shortly after we had completed the first draft of this book the Marxist historian, Neil Faulkner, entirely by coincidence, published an article with the same title, "Bread and circuses but without the bread" on the Olympics spectacle in Britain. You can read it here. Faulkner, N. 2012. "Bread and circuses but without the bread" https://yalebooks.wordpress.com/20 12/01/06/author-article-by-neil-faulkner-bread-and-circuses-but-without-the-bread/ (Accessed June 26 2012).

108 Žižek, S., 2011, "Slavoj Žižek: Capitalism with Asian values" http://www.aljazeera.com/programmes/talktojaz eera/2011/10/2011102813360731764.html (Accessed 1 May 2012)/

109 Luxemburg, R. and le Blanc, P., 2010. Socialism or Barbarism: Selected Writings, Pluto Press: London, p. 100-101

110 Breitman, G., Wald, A., and le Blanc, P., 1996, *Trotskyism in the USA* Humanities Press: New Jersey, p. 280

111 Bernstein, E., and Tudor, H., 1993, *The preconditions of socialism*, Cambridge University Press: Cambridge 112 Kouvelakis, S.,. 2011, "Facing the crisis: the strategic perplexity of the left", International Socialism Journal 130

113 Žižek, S., 2009, *First as tragedy then as farce*, Verso: London, p.7

114 Kouvelakis, S., 2011, op cit

115 Pham B, 2012, Occupy sees rebirth of American Radicalism http://anticapitalists.org/2012/05/11/occupy-rebirth-of-american-radicalism Accessed June2012

116 Harvey, D., 2012, *Rebel Cities; From the Right to the City to the Urban Revolution* Verso: London

117 Guardian, 2012. "Reading the Riots" at Guardian.co.uk (Accessed 20 July 2012).

118 For instance see The Economist. 2007 "The rise of the 'Boligarchs'", 12 August

119 Fisher, M., 2009. *Capitalism Realism*, op cit, *p.79-81*

120 Bensaïd, D., 2007. "The Return of Strategy" http://www.internationalviewpoint.org/spip.php?article1199 (Accessed 14 July 2012).

121 From an IST bulletin which was cited by Smith, M., "The broad party, the revolutionary party and the united front" in Frontlines, 02/2000

122 This is a prominent theme in the pamphlet Harvey, Keith and Stockton, Dave. eds, *Summit Sieges and Social Forums; A Rough Guide to the Anticapitalist Movement*, 2004, L5I: London

123 Tyler, P E., 2003, "A New Power in the Streets", New York Times 17 February, 2003

124 It should be noted that the combined vote of parties to the left of the Socialist Party, of 13 per cent, is still not considerably greater than the vote a similar plethora of parties won in 2002 – just over 10 per cent. This indicates that Melenchon only marginally extended the traditional left vote in France and fell well short of the breakthrough score of 17 per cent that some opinion polls in advance had anticipated.

125 For English language contributions to this debate see: Callinicos, A., 2012. "France: anti-capitalist politics in crisis" in International Socialism Journbal 134 Stanley, Jason. 2012. "France: the NPA in crisis" http://www.solidarity-us.org/site/node/3490#comm ent-2442 (Accessed 20 July 2012). Mullen, J.,2012, Socialist Alternative website, http://bit.ly/GHL9Uy (Accessed 20 July 2012).

126 Zappi, S., 2010, "Olivier Besancenot : un "nouveau Mai 68" est possible" Le Monde 15 October 2010. For a criticism see: Durand, C and Keucheyan, R, "L'isolement du NPA" 7 Febraury 2011

127 In Leplat, F. (eds), 2011, New Parties of the Left: The European experience. Resistance Books: London

128 Kouvelakis, S., 2011, op cit

129 Ibid

130 Riddell, J., 2011, "The Comintern's unknown decisions on worker's governments" http://bit.ly/N1K6ew (Accessed 23 May 2012)

131 Gramsci, A., 1971. *Selections from prison notebooks.* International Publishers: New York, p238 132 Trotsky, L., 1977, *The Death Agony of Capitalism and the task of the Fourth International today*, Pathfinder Press: New York

133 See Harvey, D., 2012, *Rebel Cities; From the Right to the City to the Urban Revolution* Verso: London

Bibliography

Bernstein E, 1993, *The preconditions of socialism*, Cambridge University Press

Bevin, Aneurin 1952 *In Place of Fear* EP Publishing: Michigan

Braudel, Fernand. 1960. "History and the Social Sciences: The Long Duration." *American Behavioral Scientist* 3

Breitman G, Wald A and LeBlanc P, 1996 *Trotskyism in the USA*, Humanities Press: New Jersey

Fisher M, 2009, *Capitalist Realism*, Zero books

Fukuyama F, 1993, *The End of History and the Last Man*, Penguin

Goethe J, 1999, *Faust part one*, Wordsworth Classics, Great Britain

Gramsci A, 1971, *Selections from prison notebooks*, International Publishers, New York

Harvey, David. 2010. *The Enigma of Capital*, Oxford University Press: Oxford

Harvey, D. 2012, *Rebel Cities; From the Right to the City to the Urban Revolution* Verso, London

Harvey, K and Stockton, D. (eds), 2004 *Summit Sieges and Social Forums; A Rough Guide to the Anticapitalist Movement*, L5I: London

Kouvelakis S, 2011, Facing the crisis: the strategic perplexity of the left, ISJ 130

Leplat F (eds), 2011, *New Parties of the Left: The European experience*, Resistance books

Luxemburg R, 2010 *Socialism or Barbarism: Selected Writings*, Pluto Press

Marcuse, Herbert, 2002 *One-Dimensional Man: Studies in the Ideology of Advanced Industrial Societ*, Routledge

Marx, Karl, 1970 *Capital Volume 1*, Lawrence and Wishhart: London

Marx, Karl. 1978 *18th Brumaire of Louis Bonaparte*, Foreign Languages Press: Beijing

Marx, Karl. 1987 *Marx and Engels Collected Works volume 28* Lawrence and Wishart: London

Mason Paul, *Why it's kicking off everywhere*, Verso

El-Mahdi R and Marfleet P, 2009 *Egypt: the Moment of Change*, Zed books

Standing, Guy. 2011 *The Precariat; The New Dangerous Class*, Bloomsbury Academic: London

Trotsky L, 1977, *The Death Agony of Capitalism and the task of the Fourth International today*, Pathfinder press

Žižek, Slavoj. 2009. *First as tragedy then as farce*, Verso: London

Contemporary culture has eliminated both the concept of the public and the figure of the intellectual. Former public spaces – both physical and cultural – are now either derelict or colonized by advertising. A cretinous anti-intellectualism presides, cheerled by expensively educated hacks in the pay of multinational corporations who reassure their bored readers that there is no need to rouse themselves from their interpassive stupor. The informal censorship internalized and propagated by the cultural workers of late capitalism generates a banal conformity that the propaganda chiefs of Stalinism could only ever have dreamt of imposing. Zer0 Books knows that another kind of discourse – intellectual without being academic, popular without being populist – is not only possible: it is already flourishing, in the regions beyond the striplit malls of so-called mass media and the neurotically bureaucratic halls of the academy. Zer0 is committed to the idea of publishing as a making public of the intellectual. It is convinced that in the unthinking, blandly consensual culture in which we live, critical and engaged theoretical reflection is more important than ever before.